Reproducible! Instant BIBLE LESSONS® For

PRETEENS

My Master's Plan

Mary J. Davis

These pages may be copied.
Permission is granted to the buyer of this book to photocopy student materials for use with Sunday school or Bible teaching classes.

An imprint of Rose Publishing, Inc.
Carson, CA
www.Rose-Publishing.com

To Larry, as always, and to our children.
Also, to all our grandchildren and great-nieces and nephews who are growing up strong in the Lord.

INSTANT BIBLE LESSONS® FOR PRETEENS: MY MASTER'S PLAN
©2014 by Mary J. Davis, seventh printing
ISBN 10: 1-58411-077-5
ISBN 13: 978-1-58411-077-4
RoseKidz® reorder# R38614
RELIGION / Christian Ministry / Youth

RoseKidz®
An imprint of Rose Publishing, Inc.
17909 Adria Maru Lane
Carson, CA 90746
www.Rose-Publishing.com

Cover Illustrator: Jennifer Kalis
Interior Illustrator: Apryl Stott

Printed in the United States of America

Contents

Introduction

Let's face it: the preteen years are a struggle. Bodily changes, emotional highs and lows, and hormones run amok are just some of the challenges of this age. The world bombards our preteens with unsavory messages at every turn. They need encouragement and opportunity to put God's Word into their hearts and minds. The best tools we can give our preteens to survive in the world today are God's Holy Word and guidance. In ***My Master's Plan***, preteens will learn that Jesus has a perfect plan for their lives and that living out His plan is the ultimate act of obedience.

Each of the first eight chapters includes a Bible story, a memory verse, alternative forms of learning the lesson theme, and a variety of activities to help reinforce the truth in the lesson. An additional chapter contains miscellaneous projects that can be used anytime throughout the study, or at the end to review the lessons.

The most exciting aspect of ***Instant Bible Lessons for Preteens*** is its flexibility. You can easily adapt these lessons to a Sunday school hour, a children's church service, a Wednesday night Bible study, or family home use. Because there is a variety of reproducible ideas from which to choose, you will enjoy creating a class session that is best for your group of students, whether large or small, beginning or advanced, active or studious, all boys/all girls/co-ed. The intriguing topics will keep your students coming back for more, week after week.

* How to Use This Book *

Each chapter begins with a Bible story. You may simply tell the story from the story page, or use the first activity to discover the lesson in a more involved way. To prepare for each lesson, duplicate the story page. Read the Bible Scriptures and the story written on the page to get a good background of the lesson you will teach your students. Jot down any thoughts that will help you teach the Bible story. Use the discussion questions to spark conversation about the Bible story.

• CHAPTER 1 •

My Master's Plan to Avoid Temptation

MEMORY VERSE

Then Jesus was led by the Spirit into the desert to be tempted by the devil.

MATTHEW 4:1

* Wise Choices *

At Jesus' request, John took Jesus into the river and lowered Him into the water. As soon as Jesus came up out of the water, a very special thing happened. Heaven opened and the Spirit of God descended like a dove. The dove came near Jesus.

"This is my Son, whom I love; with Him I am well pleased," said a voice from heaven. It was God! He wanted the world to know that Jesus was His Son, the Savior He promised to send.

To prepare for His ministry, Jesus fasted and prayed. The Holy Spirit of God led Him into the desert, where he prayed and did not eat for 40 days.

As you might expect, after 40 days without food, Jesus was hungry. Satan saw that Jesus was physically weak, hungry, and tired, and decided to play a game with Jesus.

"If you are the Son of God, tell these stones to become bread," Satan said as he appeared next to Jesus.

But Jesus knew better. "It is written: 'Man does not live on bread alone, but on every word that comes from the mouth of God,'" He said, quoting from the Scriptures.

So Satan tried again. He took Jesus to the holy city and led him to the highest point of the temple. "If you are the Son of God, jump off the cliff," Satan urged. "Surely the angels will catch you."

But Jesus again answered with God's Word. "Do not put the Lord your God to the test," He said.

One more time, Satan tried his tricks on the Son of God. He took Jesus to a very high mountain and showed him all the kingdoms of the world.

"I will give you all this, if you will bow down and worship me," Satan said.

"Away from me, Satan!" Jesus answered. "For it is written: 'Worship the Lord your God and serve him only.'"

Defeated, Satan left. Then angels came to take care of Jesus.

Jesus set some great examples for us in the way He prepared to minister. First, He was baptized to show everyone that He wanted to follow God's ways. Next, he prayed and studied God's Word so he could stand strong against temptation. As God's children, we also should be baptized, pray, and memorize Scripture so we can be good examples to others of God's love, grace, and salvation.

BASED ON MATTHEW 3:13-4:11

Discussion Questions

1. Why did God announce to everyone at Jesus' baptism that Jesus is God's Son?
2. Why did God allow Jesus to be tempted by Satan? Why does God allow us to face temptation?

group

Construct-a-cartoon

WHAT YOU NEED

- pages 8 and 9, duplicated
- scissors
- glue

WHAT TO DO

1. Give each student a copy of each pattern page.
2. Have the students cut out the word bubbles and narration strips from the instruction page.
3. Say, **You can recreate the Bible story by placing the word bubbles and narration strips in the correct spaces. Open your Bibles to Matthew 3:13–4:11 to help construct the story correctly. You may glue the pieces onto the page when you are sure you have the story assembled correctly.**

temptation

Away from me, Satan! It is written: Worship the Lord your God, and serve him only!

After not eating for 40 days you must be very hungry. If you are really the Son of God, tell these stones to become bread.

The devil took Jesus to the highest point of the temple and told him to jump because the angels would catch him.

I need to be baptized by You, yet You come to me?

This is my Son, whom I love; with Him I am well pleased.

It is written: Man does not live on bread alone, but on every word that comes from the mouth of God.

It is also written: Do not put the Lord your God to the test.

I will give You all this, if You will bow down and worship me.

Satan went away and angels came to take care of Jesus.

Jesus was led by God's Spirit into the desert to be tempted by Satan.

group

WHAT YOU NEED

- pages 10 and 11, duplicated
- pens or pencils
- scissors

WHAT TO DO

1. Say, **Everyone has been tempted. How do you handle temptation? Let's do some investigative reporting to find out how others use God's Word to help avoid the temptation to sin.** Have the students get in groups of two or three.
2. Select one student from each group to be Jesus. The other students should act as reporters interviewing Jesus about temptation. The students should then ask each other questions about temptation.
3. Fasten the reports to a bulletin board, or put them into a book to be used in the classroom throughout the "My Master's Plan" lessons.

temptation

Interview with Jesus

1. How did you feel after fasting for forty days and nights?

____

____

____

____

____

2. Why do you think God allowed you to be tempted by Satan?

____

____

____

____

____

3. Why did you use God's Word to answer the temptations?

____

____

____

____

____

4. How did it feel to defeat the devil?

____

____

____

____

____

Investigative Reporting

Are you ever tempted?

____

How do you avoid temptation?

____

____

____

How do you handle it when you know you've begun to give in to temptation?

____

____

____

Do you have a favorite Bible verse to help you avoid temptation?

____

____

____

My Own Questions to Ask:

____

____

____

____

____

Are you ever tempted?

____

How do you avoid temptation?

____

____

____

How do you handle it when you know you've begun to give in to temptation?

____

____

____

Do you have a favorite Bible verse to help you avoid temptation?

____

____

____

My Own Questions to Ask:

____

____

____

____

____

craft

* A Little Help from My Friends *

WHAT YOU NEED

- duplicated page
- scissors
- pens

WHAT TO DO

1. Give each student a pattern page.
2. Have the students cut out their cards and fold them on the center lines.
3. Say, **The card says, "I can avoid temptation with a little help from my friends." Let's all sign each other's cards to show our support in helping one another avoid temptation. You can each carry your cards in your pockets, or keep them where you can hold them when you feel you need help avoiding temptation.**

...with a little help from my friends.

I can avoid temptation....

Matthew 3:17, 4:1

temptation

* Match the Verses *

A	B
Matthew 4:4	**Deuteronomy 6:13**
Matthew 4:6	**Deuteronomy 8:3**
Matthew 4:7	**Psalm 91:11-12**
Matthew 4:10	**Deuteronomy 6:16**

puzzle

WHAT YOU NEED

- duplicated page
- pens or pencils

WHAT TO DO

1. Give each student a puzzle page.
2. Let the students work in pairs or groups.
3. Say, **Column A lists scriptures from our lesson verses in Matthew 3:13 – 4:11. Column B lists the answers Jesus gave Satan, and even includes a Scripture Satan knew from God's Word. Look up each verse in the first column. Find the verse from the second column that matches it. Draw lines between the matching verses.**
4. Have the students read the matching verses aloud.

group

WHAT YOU NEED

- duplicated page
- balloons
- large piece of cardboard
- darts
- tape
- scissors

WHAT TO DO

1. Before class, cut the phrases from the pattern page. Fold the phrases so the students can't read them while they are helping you prepare for the game.
2. Have the students help blow up balloons, one for each folded phrase. Show how to tuck a phrase inside each balloon before tying it.
3. Tape the balloons to the cardboard in an area where it is safe to throw darts.
4. Have the students take turns throwing darts. If a student breaks a balloon, he or she gets to read the phrase or word on the folded paper,

temptation

* Temptation Busters *

Bible	Friends
Prayer	Jesus' example
Holy Spirit	Example of others around me
Parents	Memorized Scriptures
Pastor	Lesson I learned at church
Sunday school teacher	Knowing God wants me to obey His Word
Grandparent	Knowing that what I do is a good or bad example for others
Conscience	

WHAT TO DO, CONTINUED

➢ then should tell how the phrase will help him or her avoid temptation. Allow for plenty of discussion for each phrase or word.

* Fuzzy Mini-poster *

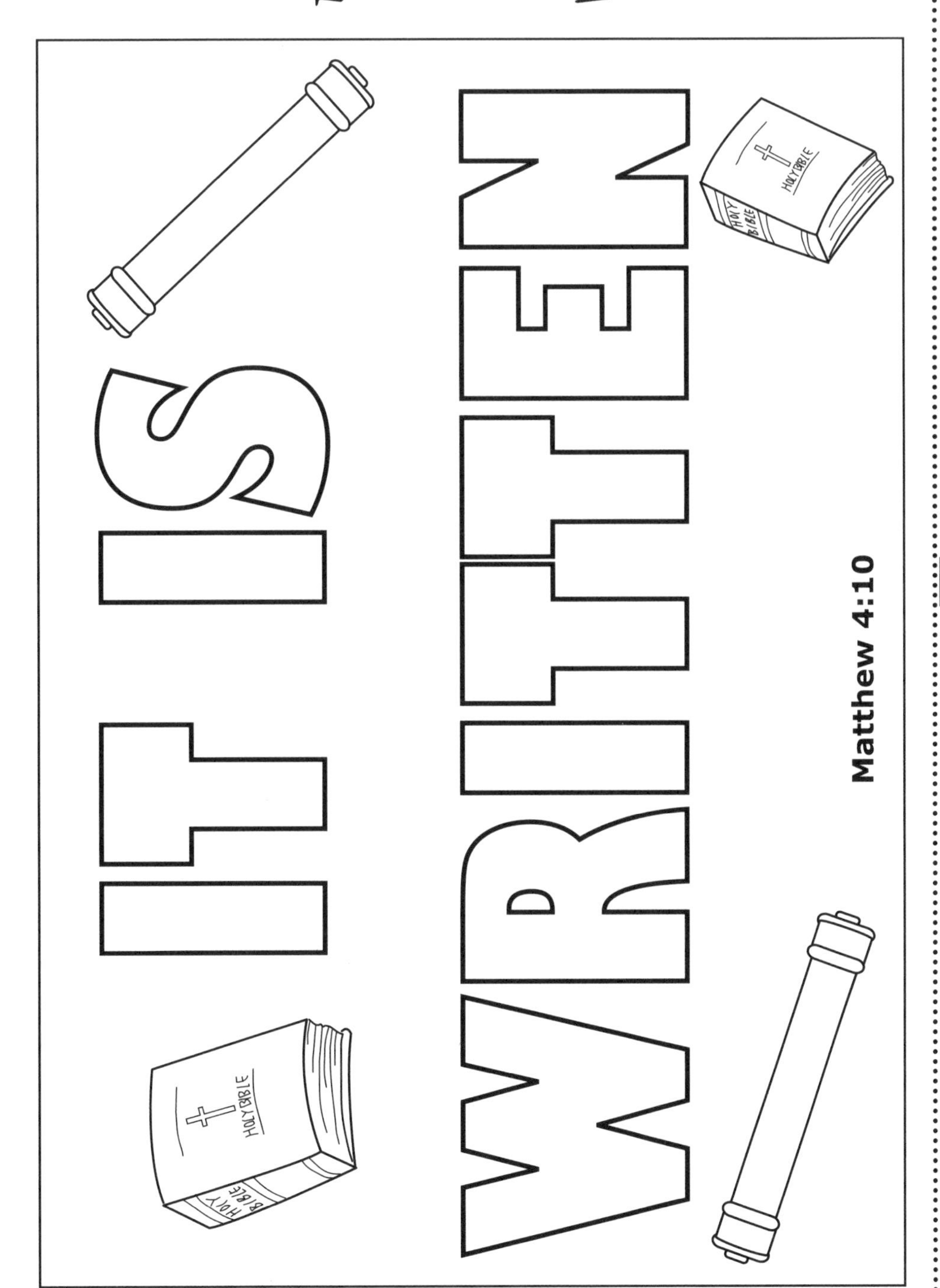

craft

WHAT YOU NEED

- duplicated page
- card stock
- markers
- glue
- chenille stems
- scissors
- cotton swabs

WHAT TO DO

1. Give each student a duplicated poster. Have the students cut out their posters.
2. Allow the students to decorate their posters with markers.
3. Glue the chenille stems to one or more letters in the poster.
4. Say, **Jesus answered temptation with these words: "It is written." We should know our Bibles well enough to answer temptation in the same way.**

group

WHAT YOU NEED

- duplicated page
- stapler
- paper

WHAT TO DO

1. Before class, duplicate the pattern and cut out two beanbags. Fold them in half on the dashed lines. Stuff the beanbags with wadded paper, and staple them closed.
2. Arrange the group into a figure-eight circle (see diagram).
3. Give two students a beanbag each. Play the game like Hot Potato.
4. Say, **Pass the "Temptation Beanbags" as quickly as you can. Each beanbag will be going the opposite direction from the other, and you will be working in a figure eight pattern. Let's try the game slowly at first, then speed it up to keep temptation on the move!**

temptation

"Avoid Temptation" Beanbags

Temptation

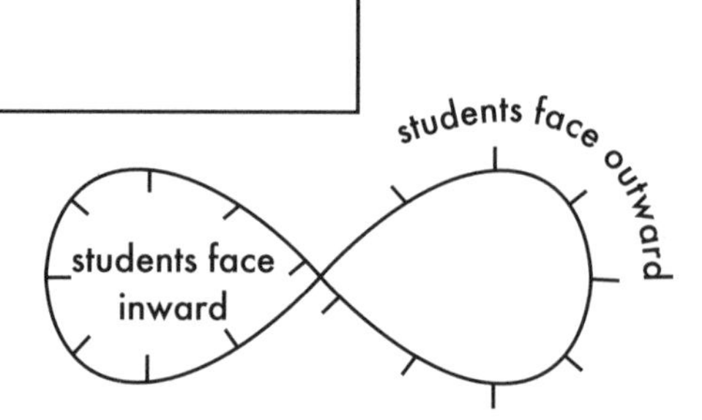

CHAPTER 2

He is All I Need

MEMORY VERSE

I am the living bread that came down from heaven. If anyone eats of this bread, he will live forever. This bread is my flesh, which I will give for the life of the world. JOHN 6:51

* "I Am" *

The book of John contains many verses in which Jesus says, "I am." These "I am" verses tell us many things about Jesus. But when we read them, we also discover that Jesus is all we need in life. Let's look at these verses.

First, Jesus says, "I am the bread of life" (John 6:48) and "I am the living bread that came down from heaven" (John 6:51). If we have the bread of life, He says, we will never go hungry, and we will live forever.

Then Jesus says, "I am the light of the world" (John 8:12). If we follow Jesus, we will never walk in darkness. He is our light in a sometimes dark and troublesome world.

Many people were shepherds during Jesus' time on earth, so He often used stories about shepherds to help people understand His teachings. The book of John has several verses about sheep and the good shepherd. "I am the good shepherd," He says, who "lays down his life for his sheep" (John 10:11). We are the sheep who will never be lost if we follow Jesus, the Good Shepherd.

Jesus also says, "I am the gate" (John 10:9). When Jesus died on the cross, He took our sins with Him. He is the gate through which we can go to heaven.

"I am the resurrection and the life," Jesus says in John 11:25-26. If we believe in Jesus, we will live forever. Even though our bodies will die, our souls never will.

Then Jesus says, "I am the vine; you are the branches" (John 15:5). Grapes grow well in the Bible lands. That's why Jesus chose a vine and branches to explain that we need to be attached to Him to grow, and to bear fruit by serving God and bringing more people to know Him. We cannot do anything good if we are separated from Jesus.

Through these "I am" verses, Jesus teaches us that He is all we need. He is the bread of life, the light, the Good Shepherd, the gate, the resurrection and the life, and the vine.

BASED ON THE VERSES LISTED

Discussion Questions

1. What are some of the things Jesus says He is in the "I am" verses?
2. Why does God want us to know that Jesus is all these things for us?

group

WHAT YOU NEED

- pages 18 and 19, duplicated
- card stock
- scissors
- rubber bands

WHAT TO DO

1. Duplicate the pattern pages to card stock for each student.
2. Have the students cut the cards apart so they have 11 verse cards each.
3. Have the students put their cards in order from 1-11.
4. The students should take turns reading the cards aloud. The entire class should follow along by looking at their own matching cards while each is being read aloud.
5. Then turn the activity into a game. Call out a number from 1 to 11 and have the first student to locate that card in his or her pile stand and read it aloud. Call out numbers as time allows.

all I need

* "I Am" Cards *

1

I am the bread of life. He who comes to me will never go hungry.

JOHN 6:35

2

I am the living bread that came down from heaven. If anyone eats of this bread, he will live forever. This bread is my flesh, which I will give for the life of the world.

JOHN 6:51

3

I am the light of the world. Whoever follows me will never walk in darkness, but will have the light of life.

JOHN 8:12

4

I am the gate for the sheep.

JOHN 10:7

5

I am the gate; whoever enters through me will be saved.

JOHN 10:9

6

I am the good shepherd. The good shepherd lays down his life for the sheep.

JOHN 10:11

7

I am the good shepherd; I know my sheep and my sheep know me.

JOHN 10:14

8

I am the resurrection and the life. He who believes in me will live, even though he dies, and whoever lives and believes in me will never die.

JOHN 11:25-26

9

I am the way and the truth and the life. No one comes to the Father except through me.

JOHN 14:6

10

I am the true vine, and my Father is the gardener.

JOHN 15:1

11

I am the vine; you are the branches. If a man remains in me and I in him, he will bear much fruit; apart from me you can do nothing.

JOHN 15:5

craft

WHAT YOU NEED

- pages 20 and 21, duplicated
- scissors
- markers
- glue sticks
- plastic sandwich bags

WHAT TO DO

1. Give each student two duplicated pages.
2. Have the students cut out and decorate the figures.
3. Show how to use a glue stick to put a light coating of glue on the backs of the stickers. Allow the stickers to dry. (If the glue is thick, the stickers might have to dry overnight.)
4. Provide plastic sandwich bags for the students to take their stickers home.
5. Say, **Jesus says, "I am" so we will know He is all we need. These stickers will remind you of the "I am" Scriptures.**

all I need

* "I Am" Stickers *

I am the light of the world. Whoever follows me will never walk in darkness, but will have the light of life.
John 8:12
I am the true vine, and my Father is the gardener.
John 15:1
I am the gate for the sheep.
John 10:7
I am the gate; whoever enters through me will be saved.
John 10:9
I am the resurrection and the life. He who believes in me will live, even though he dies, and whoever lives and believes in me will never die.
John 11:25 - 26
I am the way and the truth and the life. No one comes to the Father except through me.
John 14:6
I am the good shepherd; I know my sheep and my sheep know me.
John 10:14
I am the vine; you are the branches. If a man remains in me and I in him, he will bear much fruit; apart from me you can do nothing.
John 15:5
I am the good shepherd. The good shepherd lays down his life for the sheep.
John 10:11

craft

* "I Am" Stained Glass *

WHAT YOU NEED

- duplicated page
- transparency sheets
- scissors
- liquid leading (in squeeze bottles)
- permanent markers
- fishing line
- tape

WHAT TO DO

1. Duplicate the pattern onto a transparency sheet for each student.
2. Have the students cut the ovals from their sheets.
3. Instruct the students to use permanent markers to color the "stained glass."
4. Use the liquid leading to outline the Jesus shape and the lines forming the stained glass.
5. Allow the leading to dry overnight.
6. Show how to tape a loop of fishing line to the top of a stained glass craft. Hang the "I Am" ovals around the room.
7. Say, **Jesus said, "I am" to show us that He is all we need.**

all I need

* Write a Song *

I am the bread of life. He who comes to me will never go hungry.
—John 6:35

I am the living bread that came down from heaven. If anyone eats of this bread, he will live forever. This bread is my flesh, which I will give for the life of the world.
—John 6:51

I am the light of the world. Whoever follows me will never walk in darkness, but will have the light of life.
—John 8:12

I am the gate for the sheep.
—John 10:7

I am the gate; whoever enters through me will be saved.
—John 10:9

I am the good shepherd. The good shepherd lays down his life for the sheep.
—John 10:11

I am the good shepherd; I know my sheep and my sheep know me.
—John 10:14

I am the resurrection and the life. He who believes in me will live, even though he dies, and whoever lives and believes in me will never die.
—John 11:25-26

I am the way and the truth and the life. No one comes to the Father except through me.
—John 14:6

I am the true vine, and my Father is the gardener.
—John 15:1

I am the vine; you are the branches. If a man remains in me and I in him, he will bear much fruit; apart from me you can do nothing.
—John 15:5

express yourself

WHAT YOU NEED

- duplicated page
- plain paper
- pens or pencils

WHAT TO DO

1. Divide the class into groups. Give each group a copy of the pattern page and plain paper.
2. Say, **Jesus says, "I am." Each group can work together to write a song or poem using at least one of the "I am" verses listed on the page. You can use all or part of the verse. Use a familiar tune or make up one of your own.**
3. After all the groups have finished, let each group say or sing their song or poem.
4. Post the songs/poems on the bulletin board with a heading that says, "I Am."

group

* Vine and Branches * Mural

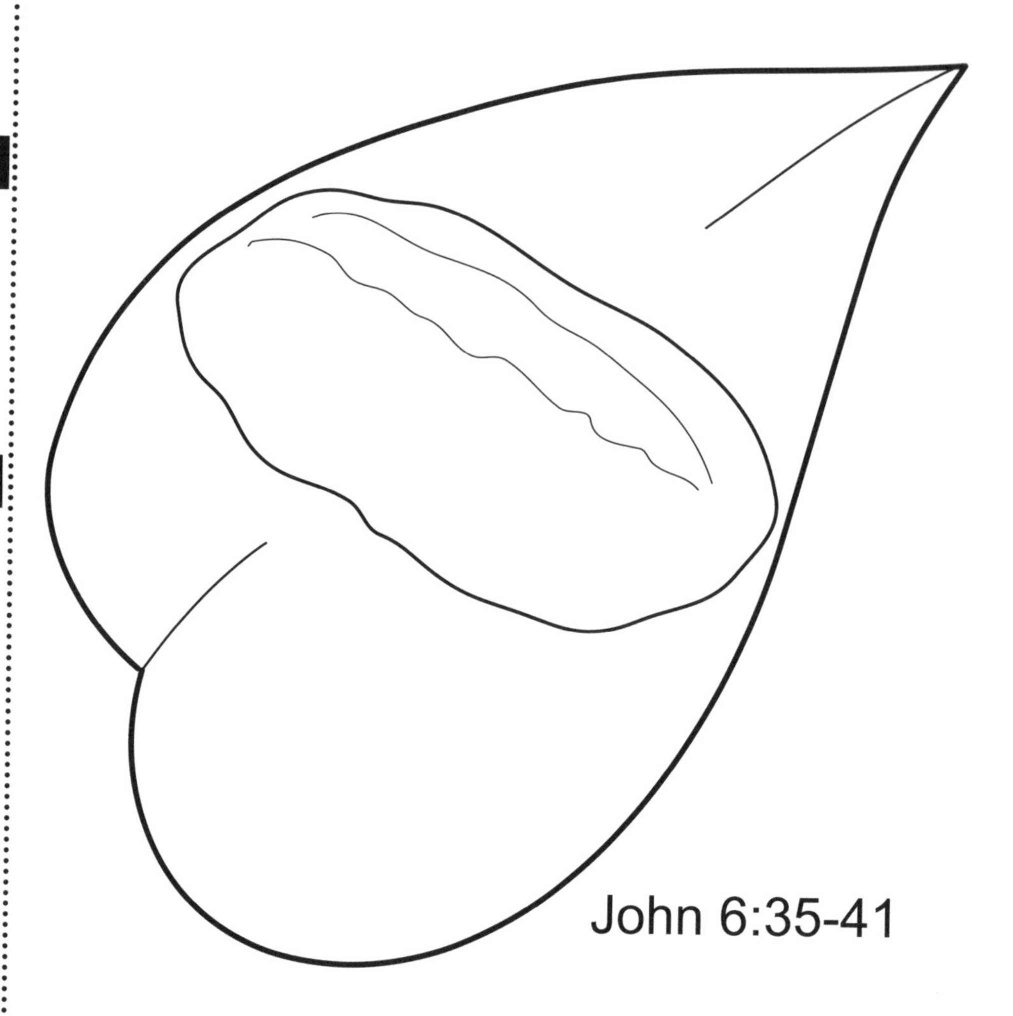

WHAT YOU NEED

- pages 24, 25, and 26, duplicated
- poster paper
- scissors
- pens or pencils
- markers
- glue

WHAT TO DO

1. Duplicate enough copies so each student will have one leaf. Spread a long length of poster paper on the floor.
2. Divide the class into six groups based on the leaves. (Two groups will get the cross picture, one will write the John 11 verses, and the other will write the John 14 verse.)
3. Say, **Each person has a picture of a leaf with a verse and a symbol. Look up the verses in your Bibles. Groups with several verses can divide the verses so that each member of your group writes one verse on his or her leaf. If** ➢

all I need

WHAT TO DO, CONTINUED

➢ **your groups only has one verse, have each member of the group write part of the verse on his or her leaf. Then glue the leaves onto the mural in the correct order so we can all read the verses as they appear in the Bible.**

4. Say, **Use markers to add vines, branches and more leaves to your part of the mural. Connect your part of the vine to the group working next to you. You also can decorate your part of the mural as you want.**
5. Say, **As we connect the pictures with the symbols by drawing vines and branches, we can see that God wants us to have the whole picture of who Jesus is: "I am all these things. I am all you need."**
6. Fasten the mural to the wall in your classroom or in a church hallway for all to enjoy.

John 8:12
John 10:14-18

John 15:1-8
John 14:6 and John 11:25-26

• CHAPTER 3 •

Jesus Demonstrates Compassion

MEMORY VERSE

When Jesus landed and saw a large crowd, he had compassion on them, because they were like sheep without a shepherd. MARK 6:34

* Christ's Compassion *

Many times in Jesus' ministry, He showed compassion to others. Jesus understood the suffering of others and wanted to make it go away. Let's look at some Bible stories that tell us about Jesus' compassion.

In Matthew 9:35-36, we find out that everywhere Jesus went, there were crowds of people who needed to be healed and wanted to hear His teachings. Jesus compassionately compared these crowds to sheep without a shepherd.

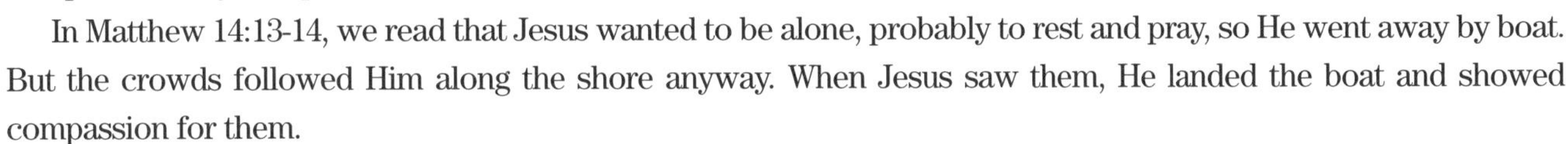

In Matthew 14:13-14, we read that Jesus wanted to be alone, probably to rest and pray, so He went away by boat. But the crowds followed Him along the shore anyway. When Jesus saw them, He landed the boat and showed compassion for them.

Jesus also had compassion for the crowds when they had no food. In Matthew 15:32 and Mark 8:2, Jesus performs a miracle to feed over 4,000 people. Jesus also fed 5,000 people in Matthew 14:15-21.

Not only did Jesus show compassion to large crowds, He also helped when there were just a few people who needed Him. Matthew 20:29-34 tells about two men who were blind. They shouted when they heard Jesus was coming near them. Jesus had compassion for them, and touched their eyes so they could see.

In Mark 1:40-42, Jesus had compassion for a leper who was an outcast. He healed him.

Jesus not only shows compassion, He encourages us to do the same. In Jesus' parable of the lost son (Luke 15:11-24), He tells about a father who showed compassion to his son who had left home. Jesus wants us know that God has compassion for those who wander away and return to Him. We should be ready to show compassion to others, even if they have wronged us.

BASED ON THE VERSES LISTED

Discussion Questions

1. Explain compassion in your own words.
2. How can we follow Jesus' example and show compassion to others?

group

WHAT YOU NEED

- pages 28 and 29, duplicated
- scissors
- index cards or note paper
- Bibles

WHAT TO DO

1. Before class, cut out the eight shapes from page 29. You will need one set for each group of students.
2. Use a different table for each group. Tape each set of verses to a table. Place index cards or note paper at each table. Cut the 15 situation strips from the instruction page for each group.
3. Divide the class into groups. Give each group a set of situation strips.
4. Say, **Each group should use your Bibles to look up the verses on the taped shapes. Write each verse on an index card and set it next to its matching shape.** ➢

compassion

* Compassion Then and Now *

My neighbors are always fighting. They aren't Christians.	Mom wants me to go to a nursing home with her and visit people I don't even know.	An elderly man in our neighborhood steals food from our garden.
I think the homeless shelter is creepy, but they need helpers to clean on Saturdays.	My big brother ran away several years ago. It broke my parents' hearts. Now he has come home and wants us to accept him back.	When we go out to dinner with my aunt's family, my little cousin always insists that I sit next to him.
My parents want to spend a holiday helping a church serve dinner to needy people.	This kid at school swears, cheats on tests, and bullies others. He made fun of me for talking about the weekend trip our youth group is going to take.	Our youth group is doing a volunteer project to help older people clean their yards. I hate hot, heavy, boring yard work.
I have saved the money to buy an MP3 player, but my friend is embarrassed about going to a school dance because he/she doesn't have any nice clothes.	My dad hasn't been in my life for many years. Now he wants to spend time with me.	Our pastor was caught taking money from the church fund. He asked our congregation to forgive him.
My little brothers are sick. I am supposed to go to a movie with friends, but Mom wants me to stay home and help her with the boys.	Our large family gatherings are uncomfortable because my parents and I are the only ones who go to church.	A teacher has asked me to help someone in our class with math. My friends are making fun of me because this person is kind of weird.

WHAT TO DO, CONTINUED

➢ 5. Have the students read their situation strips within their groups. The groups should decide which category each situation belongs in. For example: "My parents want to spend a holiday helping a church serve dinner to needy people" would go with the food basket.

6. When the groups are finished, take time to discuss the situations. Let the students discuss their ideas for things to do that fit with Jesus' acts of compassion. Say, **No answers are wrong. Any act of compassion that we show others is always the right thing to do.**

Matthew 9:36
Matthew 15:32
Matthew 14:14
Matthew 20:34
Mark 1:40-42
Mark 8:1-10
Luke 15:20
Mark 6:30-44

puzzle

WHAT YOU NEED

- duplicated page
- pens or pencils

WHAT TO DO

1. Give each student a puzzle page.
2. Say, **Using compassion is a very important lesson to learn. We've learned from our Bible lesson that Jesus taught and showed compassion in many ways. Use the words listed below the puzzle to fill in the blanks on the "compassion" acrostic. Each word is a way in which we can show compassion. Can you think of other ways?**

compassion

* Compassion Acrostic *

C ___ ___ ___

___ O ___ ___

M ___ ___ ___

___ ___ ___ P

A ___ ___ ___ ___ ___

S ___ ___ ___ ___

___ ___ S ___ ___

___ I ___ ___

___ ___ ___ ___ ___ O ___

___ N ___ ___ ___ ___

Mission	Invite	Help	Share	Accept
Meal	Care	Love	Visit	Give

* Compassionate * Project

Jesus had compassion on them.

—Matthew 20:34

Our Project

____

____

What we need

____

____

Where we will do the project

____

____

Our plan to complete the project

____

____

____

____

group

WHAT YOU NEED

- duplicated page
- pens or pencils

WHAT TO DO

1. Say, **Jesus teaches us how to show compassion to others. There are many things we can do as a class to help someone. Let's plan a volunteer project that will show compassion.**
2. Hand out several of the duplicated pages. Have the students discuss projects they could do (gently disfavor those that seem too complicated or costly).
3. Have the class vote on the ideas.
4. Plan a date to do the project. Ask parents to volunteer to help.

compassion

craft

WHAT YOU NEED

- duplicated page
- card stock
- scissors
- pens or pencils
- markers

WHAT TO DO

1. Give each student at least one pattern page duplicated to card stock.
2. Have the students cut apart the cards.
3. Say, **You can show compassion by giving someone a card. Who needs to know you care about them today? Who needs a prayer or some help from you?**
4. Have the students use markers to decorate the cards.
5. Let the students make as many cards as time allows.

compassion

* Compassion Cards *

God Loves You and So Do I!
Jesus had compassion on them.
Matthew 20:34

I Am Praying For You!
Jesus had compassion on them.
Matthew 20:34

* Compassion Skits *

Skit 1

Characters
Hannah
Mom
Friend 1
Friend 2
Narrator

Hannah: Mom, I'm going to the mall with my friends.

Mom: Oh, honey, I'm sorry. I really need your help. My boss is coming to dinner so we can discuss an important project I might get to work on. Will you please stay and help me get the house ready?

Hannah: Mom, I folded the laundry this morning. I loaded the dishwasher. Isn't that enough? I get stuck doing all the work.

Friend 1: Come on, Hannah. We're wasting time.

Friend 2: Oh, Hannah, maybe you should help your mom.

Hannah: I haven't been out with my friends in a couple of weeks. I've had to stay home and help take care of the baby while you work overtime.

Mom: This is really important to me, Hannah.

Friend 1: I'm leaving. Comin', you two?

Friend 2: Hannah, I'll stay and help you and your mom. Then maybe we can still go to the mall afterward.

Mom: Oh, that would be great, girls!

Hannah: Okay.

Friend 1: See ya later.

Friend 2: I'll be glad to help.

Narrator: Who showed compassion?

group

WHAT YOU NEED

- pages 33 and 34, duplicated

WHAT TO DO

1. Divide the class into three groups. If you have a large class, use lots of "extras" in the skits. If you have a small class, let the entire class participate in each skit.
2. Give each group one of the skits, or give each student a copy of the skit for his or her group.
3. Let the students read through their skits and decide which props they need (chairs, tables, a blanket, etc.). Allow time for students to practice their skits.
4. Have the groups perform the skits for the class. If time allows, go to another class and perform the skits.

compassion

Skit 2

Characters
Jack
Tim
Amy
Madison
Phoebe
Narrator

Amy: Hey, guys, did you hear about that new girl, Phoebe?
Jack: What about her?
Amy: I heard that…
Madison: Amy! It's not nice to gossip.
Tim: Oooo, aren't we touchy? What about that girl? She seems like a snob to me.
Amy: She doesn't have any reason to be a snob. She's…
Madison: Amy! Stop it!
Jack: Come on, Madison. Let her talk.
Tim: Yeah, we want to know what's going on.
Madison: It's just a rumor. Amy doesn't know if it's true.
Jack: True or not, tell us.
Tim: Yeah.
Amy: She's living in a homeless shelter with her mom.
Tim: Wow. She's poor and has the nerve to be snobby to me?
Madison: Maybe she's just embarrassed and doesn't want to talk to anyone.
Jack: You know, maybe Madison's right. Maybe she needs some help.
Tim: I'm not going to help some snobby girl.
Amy: I'm not going to any homeless shelter.
Madison: Maybe we could begin by being nice to her at school.
Jack: Maybe we could pretend to have too many lunch tickets and make sure she gets a lunch.
Tim: Whoa, you guys are going overboard.

Narrator: What are some ways that this group did and did not show compassion?

Skit 3

Characters
Joe
Ryan
Shelly
Josh (Joe's little brother)
Narrator

Joe: It'll just take a minute to stop by and see my little brother at the hospital. Then we can still get to the church in time for puppet practice.
Shelly: It's too bad about your brother's broken arm. I hope he gets to come home soon.
Ryan: Look at all these sick kids. Let's get out of here.
Joe: I know. We met some of them last night. Too bad when little kids get sick.
Shelly: I wish there were something we could do to help.
Ryan: I don't want to help. I just want to get out of here.
Joe: They are just little kids, Ryan. They can't help being sick.
Shelly: There's Josh. Hi, kiddo. We brought you some coloring books.
Joe: You look better today. Feeling better?
Josh: Yeah, my arm doesn't hurt as much. I got ice cream two times today!
Joe: That's great!
Shelly: Hey, Joe. I have an idea.

Narrator: A couple hours later, guess where the puppet group set up to practice?

* Journal *

Compassion: to be aware of the suffering of another, and to wish to relieve the suffering of that person.

express yourself

WHAT YOU NEED

- duplicated page
- paper
- pens or pencils

WHAT TO DO

1. Give each student a duplicated page.
2. Have someone read the definition of "compassion" aloud.
3. Say, **Write a journal page about a time when someone showed compassion to you, or when you or your family showed compassion to someone. Then write some ways you can show compassion to others.**

compassion

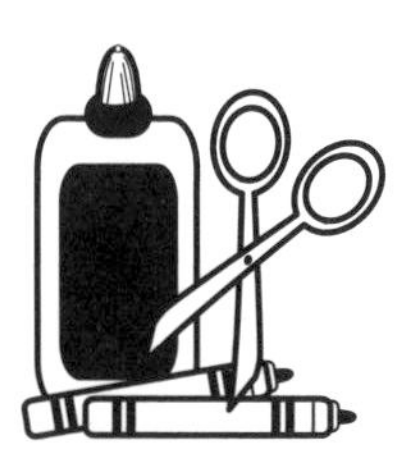

craft

* Compassion Button *

WHAT YOU NEED

- duplicated page
- plastic milk or juice caps, around 1½-inch diameter
- scissors
- glue

WHAT TO DO

1. Duplicate one compassion circle for each student.
2. Have the students cut out the circles and glue them inside the bottle caps.
3. Say, **This is an easy craft with a big meaning. Carry your compassion button in your pocket, backpack, or purse. During the day, you will see or touch your compassion button many times. Each time, think: To whom can I show more compassion? Who needs my help or encouragement right now? Who needs a prayer? Who needs to know that I and the Lord care about him or her?**

compassion

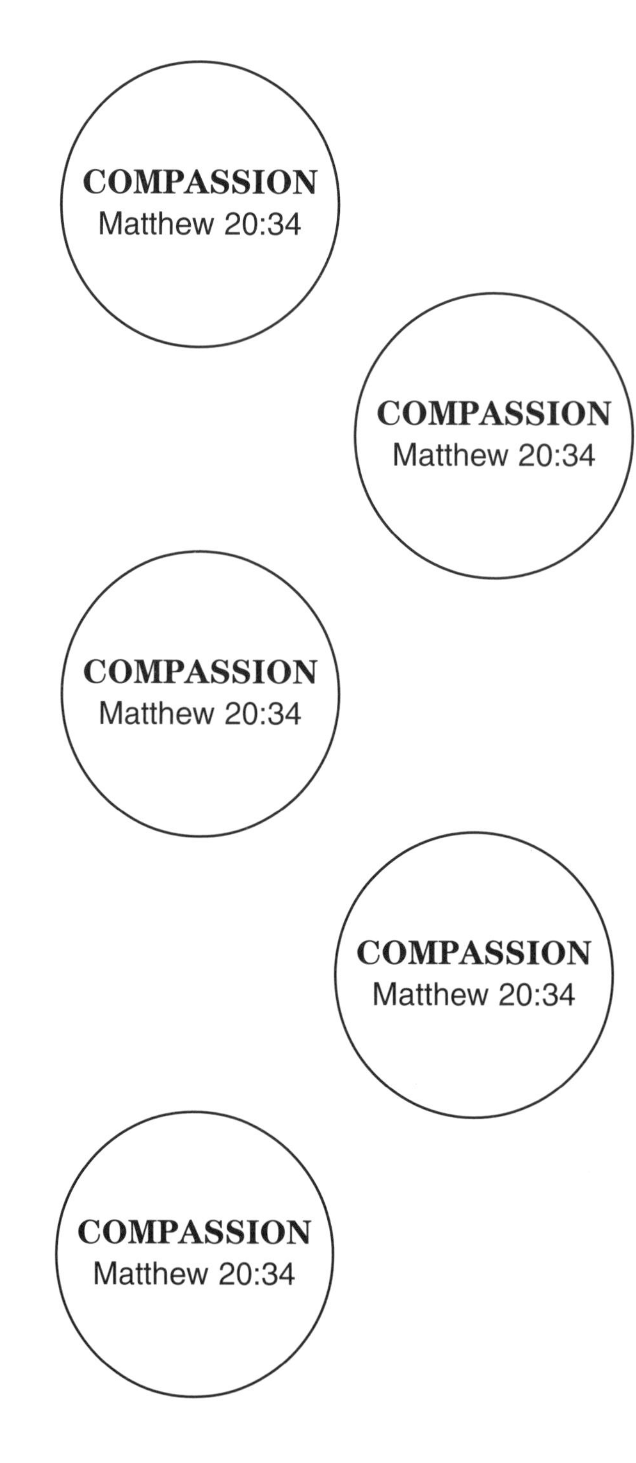

CHAPTER 4

Jesus Says Not to Worry

MEMORY VERSE

Who of you by worrying can add a single hour to his life? Since you cannot do this very little thing, why do you worry about the rest?

LUKE 12:25-26

* No Worries *

Worry. We all do it. We worry about how we look, what others think of us, and if we have enough of all the latest fashions and gadgets.

Jesus has something to teach us about worry. "Do not worry," He says. How much more plain and simple could that be? Do not worry!

Jesus tells us not to worry about our lives, what we will eat or drink, our bodies or what we will wear. He covers everything we could find to worry about.

The birds of the air don't sow or reap or store away food, yet God takes care of them. The flowers in the fields are more beautiful than anything we could ever wear ourselves, yet they don't worry. If God clothes field grass, which is here today and gone tomorrow, how much more will He care for His precious children—us? He takes such good care of us that He even knows how many hairs are on our heads!

Jesus asks, "Who of you by worrying can add a single hour to his life? Then why do you worry?"

So, when you start to worry about something, what should you focus your mind on? Jesus says, "Seek first God's kingdom and all these things will be given to you."

BASED ON LUKE 12:22-31

Discussion Questions

1. What does Jesus plainly say about worry?
2. What can be gained by worrying?

express yourself

WHAT YOU NEED

- duplicated page

WHAT TO DO

1. Give each student a duplicated page.
2. Say, **Jesus teaches us an important lesson about worry. He plainly says, "Do not worry." We're going to read the story out loud, in a round. Read each sentence when it is your turn.**
3. Have the students sit in a circle. Choose someone to begin the reading. Go around the circle with each student reading one line each.
4. Practice more than once, so the students can do the reading as smoothly as possible.

don't worry

* Round and Round Reading *

Luke 12:22-31 – Do Not Worry

Jesus said to his disciples:
"Therefore I tell you,
Do not worry about your life,
What you will eat;
Or about your body,
What you will wear.
Life is more than food,
And the body more than clothes.
Consider the ravens:
They do not sow or reap,
They have no storeroom or barn;
Yet God feeds them.
And how much more valuable you are than birds!
Who of you by worrying
Can add a single hour to his life?
Since you cannot do this very little thing,
Why do you worry about the rest?
Consider how the lilies grow.
They do not labor or spin.
Yet I tell you,
Not even Solomon in all his splendor
Was dressed like one of these.
If that is how God clothes the grass of the field,
Which is here today, and tomorrow is thrown into the fire,
How much more will he clothe you,
O you of little faith!
And do not set your heart on what you will eat or drink;
Do not worry about it.
For the pagan world runs after all such things,
And your Father knows that you need them.
But seek his kingdom,
And these things will be given to you as well."

All-too-true Story

Worry, Worry

I tossed and turned all night, worrying about the history test.
Mr. Allen is the strictest teacher, he says I don't do my best.
Still awake when the alarm went off, I jumped up out of bed.
I yelled at the dog for getting in my way; he ran and hid his head.

None of my clothes seemed just right; I worried about how I looked.
I didn't take time to eat the pancakes my mom had just cooked.
Grabbing my books, I ran out the door;
perhaps I could study before class.
Dad started the car; it sputtered some;
I worried we were out of gas.

Arriving an hour before school started, I
worried the door was locked.
Running through the grass, I tripped and
fell—the time tick-tocked.
I threw open the door and ran to
homeroom. I flung myself into
a desk.
The janitor laughed as he swept the
floor. "Mr. Allen must be giving a test."

I worried as I flipped through all my notes and tried to review the book.
My classmates came in, one by one, and at me they began to look.
My hair wasn't combed; it stood up straight; my shirt was inside out.
The other kids just shook their heads. "What are you so worried about?"

I looked at the clock; it was almost time. My eyes were fixed on the door.
The test would start any moment—I felt like fainting on the floor.
I couldn't look at the teacher. "Class," I heard a strange voice say,
"Mr. Allen has called in sick. There'll be no test today."

WHAT YOU NEED

- duplicated pages

WHAT TO DO

1. Give each student a story page.
2. Have the students take turns reading the rhyming story.
3. Say, **How many times has something similar happened to you? We all worry. We all get upset over things we wish we could change. But Jesus teaches us that we have no reason to worry. If God knows how many hairs are on our heads, if God clothes even the flowers in the fields in glorious splendor, if God knows even when a little bird falls from the sky, then why would we have any reason to worry?**
4. Have the students write about a time when they worried about something that never happened. Allow volunteers to share their stories with the class.

don't worry

craft

WHAT YOU NEED

- duplicated page
- paper
- pillow cases
- acrylic or fabric paint
- paint brushes
- scissors

WHAT TO DO

1. Give each student a stencil page, paper, and a pillow case.
2. Say, **Cut the stencils from the page to use. You also can freehand the words on the paper. Plan a design for the border of your pillowcase. Bird and flower stencils are included on the stencil page.**
3. Have the students paint the stencils on their pillowcases. Allow time for the paint to dry before the students take their pillowcases home.
4. Say, **Put your case on your pillow at home. When you get ready for bed at night, remember that Jesus said, "Do not worry."**

don't worry

Painted Pillow Cover

* No Worries * Planter

Do not worry.
Luke 12:25-26

craft

WHAT YOU NEED

- duplicated page
- flowerpots
- acrylic paints
- craft paint brushes
- glue
- potting soil
- grass seed
- scissors

WHAT TO DO

1. Give each student a pattern page and a flowerpot.
2. Have each student glue a word strip to the top edge of his or her flower-pot.
3. Have the students paint faces and ears on their pots.
4. Help the students fill their pots with soil and sprinkle in grass seed.
5. Say, **When you get home, pour a little water over the soil. Place your worry character in a sunny spot and watch the hair grow. You can cut the hair and it will continue to grow. As you enjoy your No Worries planter,**

WHAT TO DO, CONTINUED

➢ **remember that God has numbered even the hairs on your head. He doesn't want you to worry.**

don't worry

Instead of Worrying

puzzle

WHAT YOU NEED

- duplicated page
- pens or pencils

WHAT TO DO

1. Give each student a puzzle page.
2. Say, **Jesus says we should not worry and He gives us an alternative. Let's discover the word we should remember to help us not worry.**
3. Have the students write the correct word under each illustration. The five clue letters are in the bolded box of each word. They should unscramble the clue letters to finish the verse from Luke 12:28.

don't worry

Write the clue letters here: ___ ___ ___ ___ ___

Unscramble the letters to discover what we can have that will help us not to worry.

O you of little ___ ___ ___ ___ ___!

* Worry Tower *

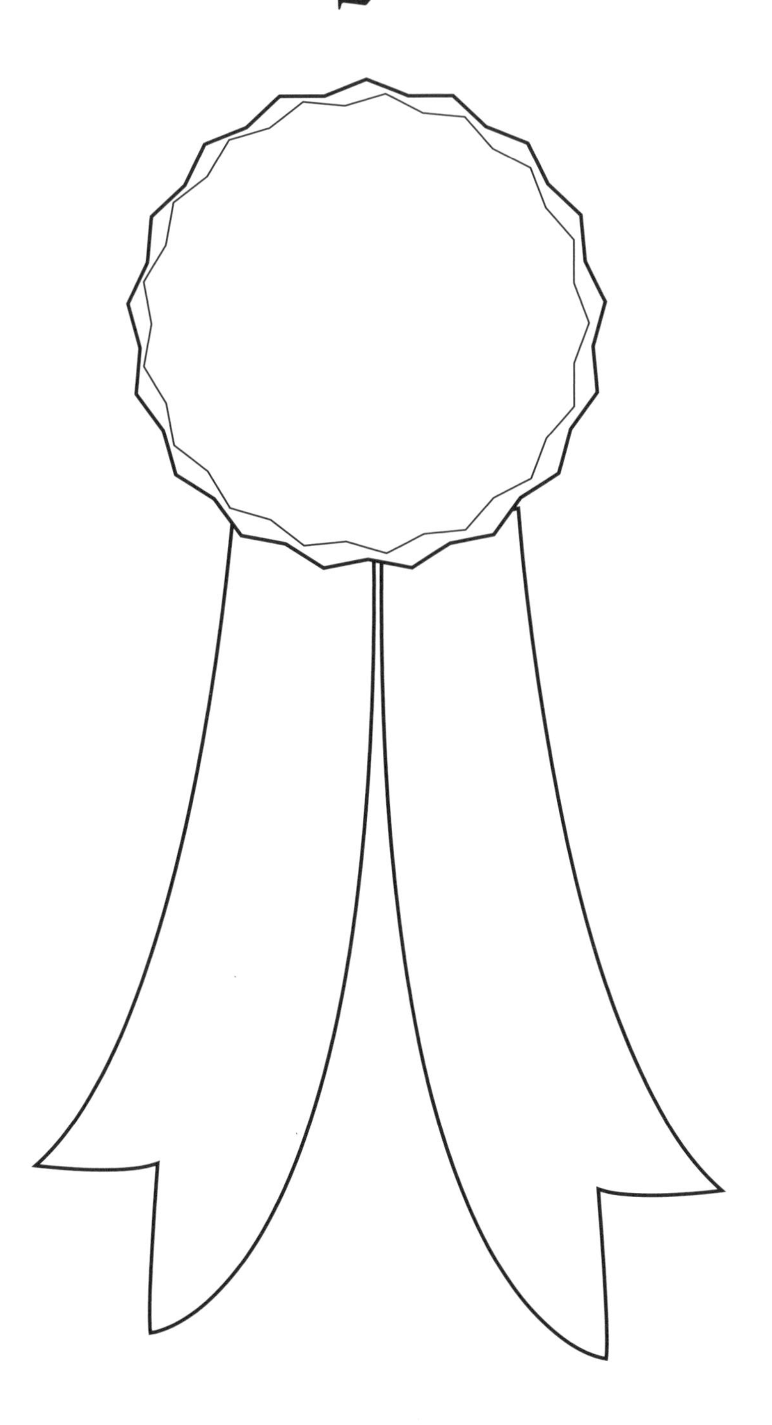

game

WHAT YOU NEED

- duplicated page
- paper or foam cups

WHAT TO DO

1. Before class, cut the winner's ribbon from the page.
2. Divide the class into two teams.
3. Place about 25 paper or foam cups at each end of the room.
4. Have each team stand next to a stack of cups.
5. Say, **When the game begins, one member of each team should take one cup and rush to the other team's area. When the first person returns to the start, the next team member should take a cup and add it to the first. Begin stacking the cups, top to top and bottom to bottom, to form a "Worry Tower." Use the unstacked cups first.**

WHAT TO DO, CONTINUED

6. Play the game until one team has gotten rid of all its cups, or until everyone has had at least one turn to run to the other team's area to help build a Worry Tower.
7. Give the winner's ribbon to the winning team, or one to everyone.

group

WHAT YOU NEED

- duplicated page
- tall snack cans with lids
- construction paper
- tape
- markers

WHAT TO DO

1. Have each student cover a snack can with decorative paper, then use markers to write "Time Capsule" on the side of the container.
2. Give each student a pattern page.
3. Say, **We worry about many things. Most things that worry us today are not important tomorrow. If we stop to think of how many things we worry about that God manages for us, we'll be able to stop worrying so much. Write down some things that are worrying you today**.
4. After the students are finished ➢

don't worry

* Time Capsule *

WORRIES to put in my TIME CAPSULE

____

____

____

____

____

____

____

____

____

____

Who of you by worrying can add a single hour to his life? Since you cannot do this very little thing, why do you worry about the rest? —**Luke 12:25-26**

WHAT TO DO, CONTINUED

➢ writing, have them roll or fold their papers and slip them inside their time capsules.

5. Say, **Take your time capsule home. Tomorrow or the next day, take out this paper and read it. Did God take away what was worrying you? How did God care for you?**
6. Encourage the students to keep their time capsules in their rooms at home and continue the activity of writing down worries and putting them inside the time capsules.

• CHAPTER 5 •

Jesus' Plan for Forgiveness

MEMORY VERSE

Forgive your brother from your heart. MATTHEW 18:35

* How Many Times? *

Sometimes we ask the silliest questions, don't we? Like, "Well, God, just how many times do You expect me to forgive someone?"

Jesus' followers were no different. They sometimes asked those silly questions, too. One disciple asked Jesus, "Lord, how many times should I forgive my brother when he sins against me? Up to seven times?"

Jesus answered, "Not seven times, but seventy-seven." Can you imagine keeping a list of everyone who makes you angry, and making a mark every time each one does something against you? You would spend your entire day just keeping track of the wrongs against you! Jesus knows we have better things to do with our time than keep lists. We should be serving God, not keeping score of the wrongs against us.

To show how we wrongly treat each other sometimes, Jesus told the parable of the unforgiving servant. Here is what He said:

A servant owed his king a lot of money. But because he couldn't pay, the king ordered that the man and his family be sold to pay the debt.

Of course, the servant begged for mercy. "Please be patient with me," he said. "I promise to pay back everything I owe you."

The king took pity on the man and forgave the whole debt. The servant didn't have to pay anything back to the king.

But that servant went right out and found someone who owed him money. He grabbed the man and began to choke him. Even though the man begged for mercy, the servant had the man thrown into prison.

The king who had forgiven the servant's debt heard about this. He was angry that the servant didn't show the same forgiveness and mercy that he had been shown. So he had the servant thrown into jail, too.

Jesus said, "This is how my heavenly father will treat each of you unless you forgive your brother from your heart."

Not only should we forgive others again and again, we should also remember that others have reason to be angry with us. We appreciate when we are forgiven, so how can we be less than forgiving to others? Has anyone caused us any more harm or heartache than we have caused God? Probably not.

Not seven times, but seventy-seven times…and then more.

BASED ON MATTHEW 18:21-35

Discussion Questions

1. What did Jesus mean when He said we should forgive "seventy-seven times"?
2. Why is it so important to Jesus that we forgive others?

WHAT YOU NEED

- Pages 46 and 47, duplicated
- simple costumes (see below)

WHAT TO DO

1. Give each student a duplicated page.
2. Assign parts for the skit. If you have a large class, put the students in groups and let each group act out the skit.
3. Encourage the students to wear simple costumes made from robes and scarf head-dresses.
4. Have the students act out the skit at least once. Perform the skit for another class.

forgiveness

* How Many Times? *

Characters:

Jesus
Peter
various disciples
King
servant
servant's friend
other servants
prison guards

Scene 1

Jesus, Peter, and other disciples

Peter: Lord, how many times should I forgive my brother when he sins against me? Up to seven times?

Other disciples gather close to Jesus and listen carefully to hear His answer.

Jesus: I tell you, not seven times, but 77 times.

Peter and other disciples look surprised.

Jesus: The kingdom of heaven is like a king who wanted to settle accounts with his servants…

Peter and other disciples follow Jesus off stage.

Scene 2

King, Servant, Servant's Friend, prison guards, other servants

King: Bring me the next one.

Prison guards bring servant before the king.

King: You owe me a thousand talents! How do you expect to repay me?

Servant: I have no money to pay you.

King: Have him thrown into prison—him and his entire family!

Prison guards grab the man and start to drag him away.

Servant [falls to knees]: Please be patient with me. I will pay back everything. Please don't put me in prison. Please spare my family!

King [*rubs chin as though thinking*]: You don't have to pay me back. You can go free.

Servant runs to other end of stage.

Servant's friend walks on stage.

Servant [*grabs his friend and starts to choke him*]: You owe me 100 denarii! Pay me back what you owe me!

Servant's friend: Please be patient with me. I don't have the money now. I will pay you back! Please be patient.

Servant: I will not be patient with you. You owe me money. Now you will go to prison because of your debt.

Servant drags the man to the prison guards and has him hauled off to prison.

Other servants see what happens and run to tell the king.

King: Bring the man before me!

Prison guards drag the servant to the king.

King: You wicked servant! I forgave all of your debt because you begged me. You should have had mercy on your friend just as I had on you.

Servant has no answer for the king.

King: Drag him off to prison!

Guards drag the man away. King and all other characters leave the stage.

Jesus, Peter, and other disciples walk back onto stage.

Peter and others listen while Jesus talks.

Jesus: This is how My heavenly Father will treat each of you unless you forgive your brother from the heart.

Peter and disciples follow Jesus off stage.

WHAT YOU NEED

- duplicated page
- craft foam
- scissors
- glue
- fishing line
- tape

WHAT TO DO

1. Give each student a pattern page. Have the students cut out the letters and trace them onto craft foam. They will need more than one of some of the letters.
2. Show how to arrange the foam letters in a collage to form the verse printed on the pattern page.
3. When the students are satisfied with their arrangements, they should glue the letters together.
4. After the glue is dried, each student should tape a loop of fishing line to the top edge of his or her collage for a hanger.
6. Say, **You can hang your verse collage at home to remind you that you should forgive from the heart.**

forgiveness

* Memory Verse * Collage

* Seventy-seven Times *

Forgave brother for spilling soda on math book. Move two spaces.

Yelled at mother for forgetting to sign field trip permission slip. Move back 3 spaces.

Forgave teacher for being unfair on a test. Move ahead 2 spaces.

Forgave friend who lost favorite CD. Move ahead 3 spaces.

Forgave classmate who stole lunch money. Move ahead 2 spaces.

Told friend she's no longer friend because of gossiping. Move back 3 spaces.

Lost temper at little brother for eavesdropping on phone. Move back 3 spaces.

Asked a friend for forgiveness, then got angry at another for the same reason. Go back 2 spaces.

Prayed for help to forgive someone who really hurt me. Move ahead 5 spaces.

Told God I could never forgive a relative for hurting my family. Move back 3 spaces.

Wrote a mean letter to someone who keeps talking about me. Go back 3 spaces.

Stole a video game from someone who lost my game. Move back 5 spaces.

Got a friend in trouble just because he got me in trouble last week. Move back 2 spaces.

Lied about someone to keep my friends from liking him or her. Move back 4 spaces.

Remembered I'm not supposed to keep track of wrongs against me. Move ahead 1 space.

Prayed for forgiveness for hurting someone. Move ahead 3 spaces.

Told someone he or she will never be my friend again. Go back 2 spaces.

Admitted my faults to someone who needed to know he or she is forgiven. Move ahead 5 spaces.

games

WHAT YOU NEED

- pages 49, 50, and 51, duplicated
- card stock
- index cards
- scissors
- glue
- plastic soda bottle caps
- tape

WHAT TO DO

1. Before class, cut the strips from the instruction page. Glue each strip to an index card. Duplicate the game board pages to card stock. Tape the two game board pieces together.
2. If you have a large class, make one game set for every five or six students.
3. Place the game board on a table. Stack the index cards face-down and place them where all the players can reach them.
4. Have each student choose a bottle cap as a playing piece.
5. Let the students take turns drawing cards, reading the instructions out

WHAT TO DO, CONTINUED

loud, and moving their game pieces as the cards direct.

6. Say, **There are 77 spaces on the game board. Jesus says we should forgive others not seven times, but seventy-seven times.**

Start
LOSE A TURN
Tape Here
LOSE A TURN
Tape Here
TAKE ANOTHER TURN
TAKE ANOTHER TURN
Tape Here

Tape Here
TAKE ANOTHER TURN
LOSE A TURN
Tape Here
TAKE ANOTHER TURN
LOSE A TURN
Tape Here
TAKE ANOTHER TURN
True Forgiver

puzzle

WHAT YOU NEED

- duplicated page
- plain paper
- scissors
- glue or glue sticks

WHAT TO DO

1. Give each student a puzzle page and sheet of plain paper.
2. Say, **The puzzle contains the word "forgive" eight times. Cut the puzzle pieces from the page. Assemble the puzzle on the plain paper in a rectangular shape. When you figure out how to assemble the puzzle, you can glue the pieces onto the plain paper.**
3. When everyone is finished, say, **It took a little time and effort to cut and assemble the puzzle. God wants us to take time and effort to forgive others, too.**

forgiveness

* Time for * Forgiveness

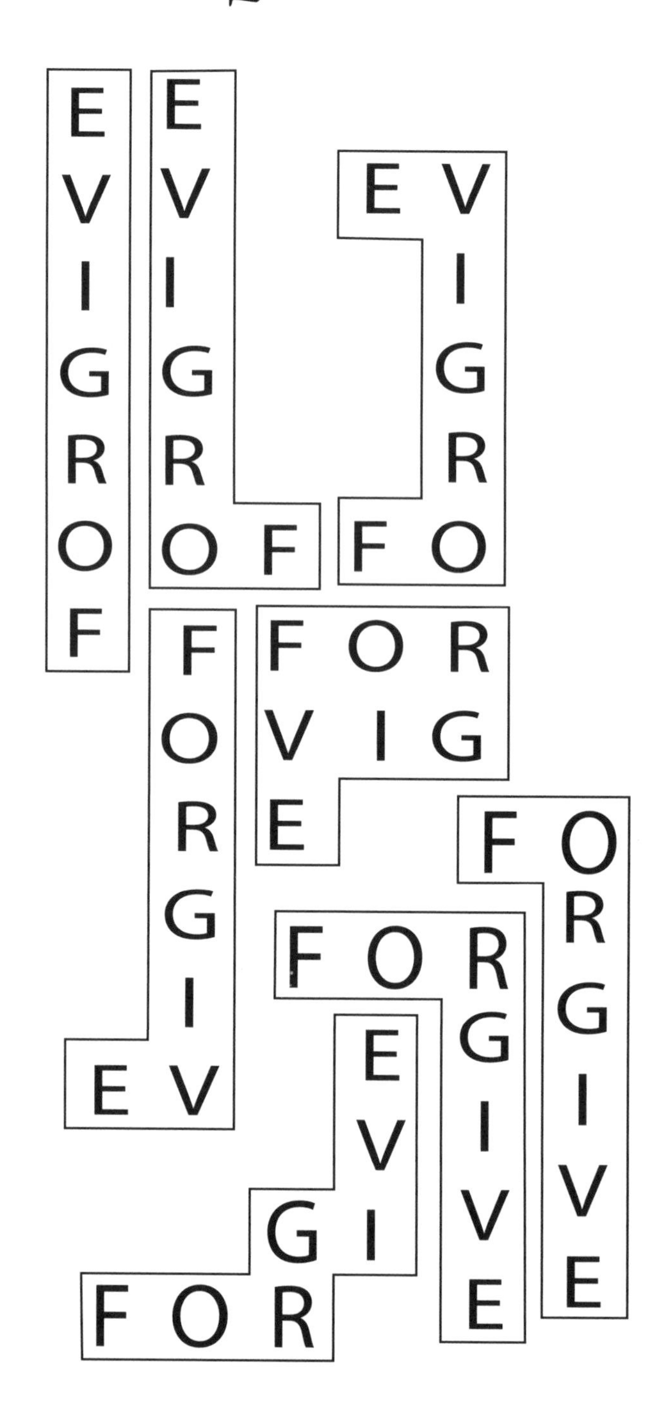

* Door Decoration *

FORGIVENESS
PRACTICED
HERE

craft

WHAT YOU NEED

- duplicated page
- foam or cardboard
- foil gift wrap
- seed beads
- glue
- scissors
- tape
- fishing line

WHAT TO DO

1. Give each student a duplicated page.
2. Have the students trace their cardboard or foam shapes onto foil gift wrap, cut out the shapes and glue them onto the cardboard or foam for colorful backgrounds.
3. Show how to tape a loop of fishing line to the top of a door sign for a hanger.
4. Have each student cut the rectangle from his or her pattern page and glue it onto the cardboard or foam piece.
5. Show how to spread glue inside the words on the verse rectangle and fill the glued areas ➤

WHAT TO DO, CONTINUED

➤ with seed beads (press down the beads so they stick well in the glue).

6. Let the projects dry before hanging them in your classroom or allowing students to take theirs home.

think

WHAT YOU NEED

- duplicated page
- pens or pencils

WHAT TO DO

1. Give each student a duplicated page.
2. Say, **Write about how you feel when you have wronged someone and that person forgives you. Or write about how it feels to be forgiven by God. Then write about why it is important for you to "do unto others" as you would like them to do unto you. Can you feel good about being forgiven when you don't forgive others?**

forgiveness

* Do Unto Others *

How I feel when I am forgiven by others:

____

____

____

____

How I feel when I know God forgives me:

____

____

____

____

Why it is important to "do unto others" and forgive others as I would like them to forgive me:

____

____

____

____

• CHAPTER 6 •

Jesus Teaches Us Not to Judge Others

MEMORY VERSE

Do not judge, and you will not be judged. Do not condemn, and you will not be condemned. LUKE 6:37

* What's in My Eye? *

Jesus teaches us not to judge others. "Do not judge," He says, "and you will not be judged. Do not condemn and you will not be condemned."

But what do these things mean? We hear these words often, but we need to understand them so we know what we should do and not do to others.

To judge means to criticize others. To condemn means to rebuke or express strong disapproval. How do we do those things to those around us? Jesus gives us a great example.

`"Why do you look at the speck of sawdust in your brother's eye and pay no attention to the plank in your own eye?" He says. "How can you say to your brother, 'Brother, let me take the speck out of your eye,' when you yourself fail to see the plank in your own eye? You hypocrite, first take the plank out of your eye, and then you will see clearly to remove the speck from your brother's eye."

By judging others, we criticize them and then treat them differently than Jesus wants us to. By condemning others, we show our strong disapproval. We tend to push those people away from us and act like we are better than they are.

But we are no better than those we ourselves judge! We have faults, too. We sin, too. We hurt others, too.

If we insist on focusing on the faults of others and don't recognize our own faults, Jesus says we are hypocrites. A hypocrite is someone who tries to make others believe something that he or she does not believe himself. A hypocrite talks falsely. You might say that a hypocrite sees the wrong in others, but not in himself.

"Do not judge others," Jesus says. "Do not condemn others." After all, we have enough faults of our own to work on rather than going around pointing out the faults of others!.

BASED ON LUKE 6:37-42; MATTHEW 7:1-5

Discussion Questions

1. Why does Jesus want us to avoid judging others?
2. When you are tempted to point out someone's fault, what can you do instead?

skit

WHAT YOU NEED

- pages 56, 57, and 58, duplicated
- picture of Jesus
- table and chair

WHAT TO DO

1. Say, **Jesus says that we should not judge or condemn others.**
2. Say, **We are going to learn more about judging and condemning by having some mock trials. In our mock trials, Jesus will be the ultimate Judge.**
3. Choose students to perform each skit. (After the skits are completed, the students will have heard the Matthew and Luke verses about judging, condemning, and "a speck in your brother's eye" four times!)
4. Allow time for questions. Reread the definitions if some students don't seem to understand the concepts of judging and condemning others.

don't judge

Mock Court

Definitions:

To JUDGE means to criticize, form an opinion, pass a sentence, or condemn.

To CONDEMN means to rebuke, express strong disapproval of, or pronounce judgement against someone.

Characters:

Accused

Accuser

Jesus **(have a student stand behind a picture of Jesus and do the "narrator" part in each skit)**

Witnesses

Verse Reader

Set up a stage with a chair for the accused; a table with Jesus' picture on it, and room for the
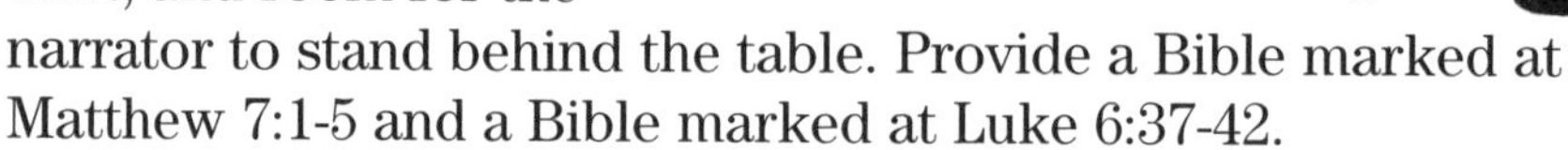
narrator to stand behind the table. Provide a Bible marked at Matthew 7:1-5 and a Bible marked at Luke 6:37-42.

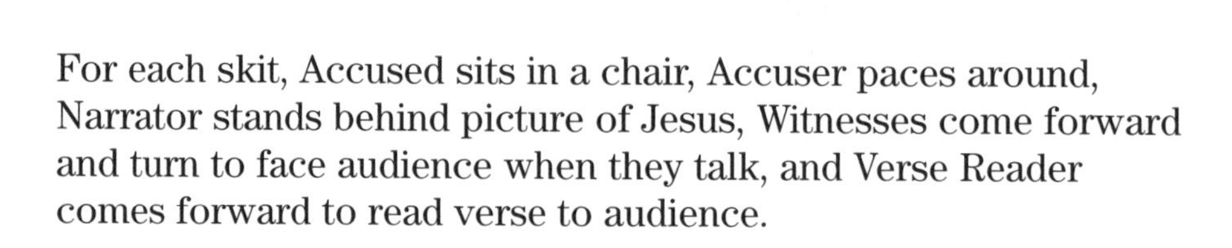
For each skit, Accused sits in a chair, Accuser paces around, Narrator stands behind picture of Jesus, Witnesses come forward and turn to face audience when they talk, and Verse Reader comes forward to read verse to audience.

Skit 1: Test Cheating

Accuser: I saw this boy cheating on a test. He copied some of my answers.

Witness 1: He copied some of my answers, too.

Witness 2: I saw him looking at the papers of both people. He definitely copied answers.

Accuser: See, he is guilty! He cannot be trusted. How can I be friends with a cheater? How can any of us be friends with a cheater?

Accused: It was a very hard test. I only copied because I knew these two had the answers written on their arms.

Witness 2: I saw the writing on their arms.

Witness 3: Well then, how can we trust these two? They are just as bad as the one who is accused of copying answers!

Accused: Yeah, these two don't deserve to have any friends either! They cannot be trusted!

Narrator: Hypocrites! You each are judging the other. Everyone who cheated is wrong. You, the Accuser, are condemning someone for doing exactly what you did. You, the Accused, are condemning the people from whom you copied your answers. A hypocrite tries to get someone to believe something that he doesn't believe himself. You knew you were guilty of the same thing of which you were accusing the others. Hypocrites!

Verse reader: (*reads Luke 6:37 and 6:41:42*)

Skit 2: Broken Promise

Accuser: My mom sits here on this chair, guilty! She broke an important promise to me.

Accused: It's true. I broke a promise.

Accuser: Not just any promise. We were going on a weekend trip to an amusement park. I worked hard to bring my grades up. And then Mom broke her promise, and we didn't go.

Accused: I said we'd reschedule the trip. I got called in to work. I couldn't help it.

Accuser: It doesn't matter now! My weekend was ruined. I can't trust my mom's promises anymore.

Witness 1: I am this (boy or girl's) conscience. I am a witness to some broken promises that (he/she) thinks nobody knows about.

Accuser: Wait a minute! I didn't call this witness.

Witness 1: I am your conscience. I don't have to be called for a witness. Now, do you care to admit to the time you promised your mom you wouldn't leave the library? Do you want to tell your mom you were at the mall with friends?

Accuser: That isn't the same.

Witness 2: I was with you at the mall. You didn't care about your promise to your mom, as long as you didn't get caught.

Witness 1: And there are more…many, many more. Shall I go on?

Accuser: No, I don't want to talk about it. My mom broke an important promise and that's all you need to hear!

Narrator: You are a perfect example of one who points out the little speck of sawdust in someone's eye, while you can barely see around that great big plank of wood in your own eye. You dare to judge your mom for a promise you feel she broke, when you are the one who has truly broken some promises! Take that big log out of your own eye before you start pointing at little specks in someone else's eye!

Verse reader: (*reads Matthew 7:1:5*)

Skit 3: The Missing Video Game

Accuser: I am here today to accuse this person of lying. She told me she didn't have my favorite video game. Yet her little brother told me it was in her backpack.

Witness 1: I found the video game in my sister's backpack. She said she borrowed it and was going to return it.

Witness 2: She brought that video game to my house and we played it together.

Accuser: Guilty! No other witnesses needed!

Accused: I took that video game. I admit it. But I don't own any video games, and my friend wouldn't loan it to me. I was going to give it back.

Accuser: See, she's guilty! She's no longer my friend. She doesn't deserve to have any friends!

Witness 3 to Accuser: Where did you get that video game?

Accuser: That's none of your business. It is my game!

Witness 4 to Accuser: I heard you tell someone at school that you stole the game from the store.

Witness 3: I heard you say the same thing. You were bragging about getting away with stealing that game!

Narrator (*standing behind picture of Jesus*): You are a hypocrite! You accused someone of taking the game from you. You stole it from a store. You are pointing to a speck in someone's eye when you have a plank in your own eye. How would you feel if your friends condemned you just like you condemned this person?

Verse reader: (*reads Luke 6:37 and Luke 6:41:42*)

Skit 4: Loose Tongues

Accuser: This person has been gossiping about me. I have proof.

Witness 1: I heard her say some things about the Accuser.

Witness 2: She told me she heard the Accuser say that this other girl in class is…well, I can't even repeat the words, they are so bad.

Accuser: See, this proves that this person has been spreading gossip about me.

Accused: I admit it. I did say those things about you. But you said some pretty bad things about my friend.

Accuser: What? Me?

Witness 3: It's true. I heard the Accuser saying those things about the other girl in our class. He was angry because the girl got a better grade in math class.

Accused: I heard the Accuser talk about my friend. My friend didn't deserve to be talked about.

Narrator: You are both guilty. You are both hypocrites. You spread gossip about other people, accusing them of spreading gossip. How silly is that?

Verse Reader: (*reads Matthew 7:1:5*)

* Sawdust Plaques *

Sawdust Modeling Dough

1 cup sawdust
1 cup glue
Mix together, then mold into a shape.
Air dry several days, or bake at 200° Fahrenheit for 2 hours.
Spray with clear spray paint to make shiny.

craft

WHAT YOU NEED

- duplicated page
- sawdust
- glue
- wax paper
- measuring cups
- plastic bowls
- mixing spoons
- scissors
- clear spray paint (optional)

WHAT TO DO

1. Give each student a pattern page. Have the students cut out the verse shapes.
2. Say, **Jesus tells us not to point out specks of sawdust in our brothers' eyes, when we have planks of wood in our own eyes. Sawdust, of course, is very small. We're going to use sawdust modeling dough, then make plaques from the dough to remind us not to judge others.**
3. Each student should measure one cup of sawdust

WHAT TO DO, CONTINUED

and one cup of glue, and place both ingredients in a plastic bowl.

4. Have the students mix the sawdust and glue until it is like modeling dough, then pour the dough onto wax paper.
5. Show how to use the dough to make a plaque (any shape: oval, rectangle, square, etc.).
6. The dough will air-dry in a few days, but it also can be dried by baking at 200 degrees F for about two hours.
7. Have the students spray their dried plaques with clear spray paint and glue the verse shapes onto their plaques.

don't judge

craft

WHAT YOU NEED

- duplicated page
- marker

WHAT TO DO

1. Give each student a poster.
2. Say, **We all tend to judge others and forget that we, too, do the same things. We break promises, hurt others' feelings, and commit sins. Yet, we are quick to tell others about their faults, while forgetting that we all have faults.**
3. Have the students color the posters with markers.
4. Say, **On the blank lines, write some things for which you tend to judge others while you do the same things.** Suggest: Dishonesty, gossip, cheat, lie, disobey parents.
5. Allow time for the students to discuss the things they have written on their posters.

don't judge

* Judging Others Poster *

____

____

____

____

"Do not judge, and you will not be judged. Do not condemn, and you will not be condemned. Forgive, and you will be forgiven. Why do you look at the speck of sawdust in your brother's eye and pay no attention to the plank in your own eye? How can you say to your brother, 'Brother, let me take the speck out of your eye,' when you yourself fail to see the plank in your own eye? You hypocrite, first take the plank out of your eye, and then you will see clearly to remove the speck from your brother's eye." *—Luke 6:37, 41-42*

* Discover More *

Put A's in spaces 13, 34
Put E's in spaces 10, 12, 17, 23, 31, 33, 38
Put I's in spaces 5, 24, 27
Put O's in spaces 2, 19, 41, 43
Put U's in spaces 15, 20, 21, 36, 44

Put B in space 30
Put D in space 39
Put F in space 1
Put H's in spaces 7, 9
Put L's in spaces 28, 29
Put M's in spaces 11, 32

Put R's in spaces 3, 16, 37
Put S's in spaces 14, 22, 35
Put T's in spaces 6, 8, 25, 40
Put W's in spaces 4, 26
Put Y's in spaces 18, 42

__ __ __   __ __ __ __   __ __ __   __ __ __ __ __ __ __
1 2 3   4 5 6 7   8 9 10   11 12 13 14 15 16 17

__ __ __   __ __ __,   __ __   __ __ __ __   __ __
18 19 20   21 22 23,   24 25   26 27 28 29   30 31

__ __ __ __ __ __ __ __   __ __   __ __ __. *—Luke 6:38*
32 33 34 35 36 37 38 39   40 41   42 43 44

puzzle

WHAT YOU NEED

- duplicated page
- pens or pencils

WHAT TO DO

1. Give each student a puzzle page.
2. Say, **We can learn more about what Jesus says about judging and condemning others. Follow the directions to place letters in the correct spaces. Then read the verse. It is the last sentence in Luke 6:38.**
3. Have the students discuss what this statement means in relationship to the judging and condemning verses they have learned.

don't judge

craft

* Back Atcha * Mirror

WHAT YOU NEED

- duplicated page
- colored card stock
- small mirrors (up to 5 inches square) or junk CDs
- 8″x10″ cardboard
- paints
- craft paint brushes
- glue
- scissors
- pencils

WHAT TO DO

1. Give each student a pattern page duplicated to colored card stock and an 8″ x 10″ piece of cardboard.
2. Say, **We are going to make a mirror that reminds us that things can come "back atcha." After you cut the rectangle from the pattern page, decide how you want to place it on your cardboard piece. Trace around the rectangle where you plan to glue it later.** ➢

WHAT TO DO, CONTINUED

➢ 3. Have each student paint their cardboard, leaving the rectangle blank.
4. After the paint is dry, have the students glue their card stock rectangles in place on their cardboard rectangles.
5. Show how to glue a mirror or a junk CD (shiny side out) onto the marked area of the rectangle.
6. Say, **Put your mirror in your room at home. Each time you look at yourself in the mirror, remember that how you judge or condemn others will come "back atcha."**

don't judge

The No Zone

group

WHAT YOU NEED

- pages 63 and 64, duplicated
- red plastic plates
- red wide-tip markers
- glue
- scissors
- fishing line
- tape

WHAT TO DO

1. Give each student two copies of each duplicated page.
2. Say, **We are going to turn our classroom into a No Judging and No Condemning zone. If we remember to treat each other with respect and leave out the judging and condemning, we will create a habit of eliminating judging and condemning from our lives. Let's fill the room with "No Judging" and "No Condemning" zone signs.**

WHAT TO DO, CONTINUED

3. Have the students cut the circles from the pages.
4. Have them color the crossed-out areas of the signs with red markers.
5. Have the students glue their circles to red plastic plates, one on the front and one on the back of each plate's center.
6. Let the students help you use fishing line and tape to hang the signs around the room.

don't judge

CONDEMN
OTHERS

• CHAPTER 7 •

Jesus: The Way

MEMORY VERSE

For we know that our old self was crucified with him so that the body of sin might be done away with, that we should no longer be slaves to sin—because anyone who has died has been freed from sin. Now if we died with Christ, we believe that we will also live with him.

ROMANS 6:6-8

* God's Plan *

God sent His Son, Jesus, to earth to show us how to live. God also planned that Jesus would die on a cross to save us from our sins. Everything that Jesus did and that happened to Him was part of God's plan. Nothing was a coincidence or an accident. Let's review what happened during Jesus' last days.

Judas, one of Jesus' disciples, knew that the chief priests were planning to capture and kill Jesus. So he went to these men and asked, "What will you give me if I hand Him over to you?" They offered Judas 30 pieces of silver to betray Jesus.

Judas led soldiers to Jesus. He was arrested and taken to the high priest. The priests questioned Jesus and mocked Him. They spat in Jesus' face and hit Him.

Then Jesus was turned over to Pilate, the governor. Jesus was tried and turned over to the angry soldiers. The soldiers beat and whipped Jesus. They stripped Him and put a crown of thorns on His head, and led Him away to crucify Him.

At a hill named Golgotha, the soldiers nailed Jesus to a cross. They gambled away His clothing and mocked Him. As Jesus neared death, darkness came over the earth. The temple curtain was torn from top to bottom. Then the earth shook and the rocks split. Tombs broke open and bodies of many people were raised to life.

Jesus was buried in a tomb. A large stone was put in front of the tomb so that the disciples could not steal Jesus' body. Soldiers guarded the tomb.

After three days, some women who were Jesus' followers came to the tomb. There was a violent earthquake and the stone rolled away from the tomb. The women were afraid.

Then they saw an angel sitting on the stone. "Do not be afraid," the angel said. "The one you are looking for is Jesus. He is not here. He has risen!"

BASED ON MATTHEW CHAPTERS 26-28

Discussion Questions

1. Why did Judas betray Jesus? What are some ways we betray Jesus today?
2. Why did Jesus disappear from the tomb? Why does His resurrection mean to you?

group

* Salvation * Treasure Hunt

WHAT YOU NEED

- pages 66, 67, and 68, duplicated
- scissors

WHAT TO DO

1. Before class, cut out the 12 crosses and hide them around the room.
2. Say, **Jesus, taught us about salvation. Twelve crosses are hidden around the room.**
3. After all the crosses have been found, divide the class into six groups.
4. Say, **Each group should take a cross and open a Bible. Look up the Scriptures in your Bibles. Discuss the important points in your Scriptures. Be prepared to tell your part of the story to the class.**
5. Beginning with the first cross, have each group tell its part of the Easter story.
6. After all groups have had a turn, have the class read the memory verse together out loud from Romans 6:6-8.

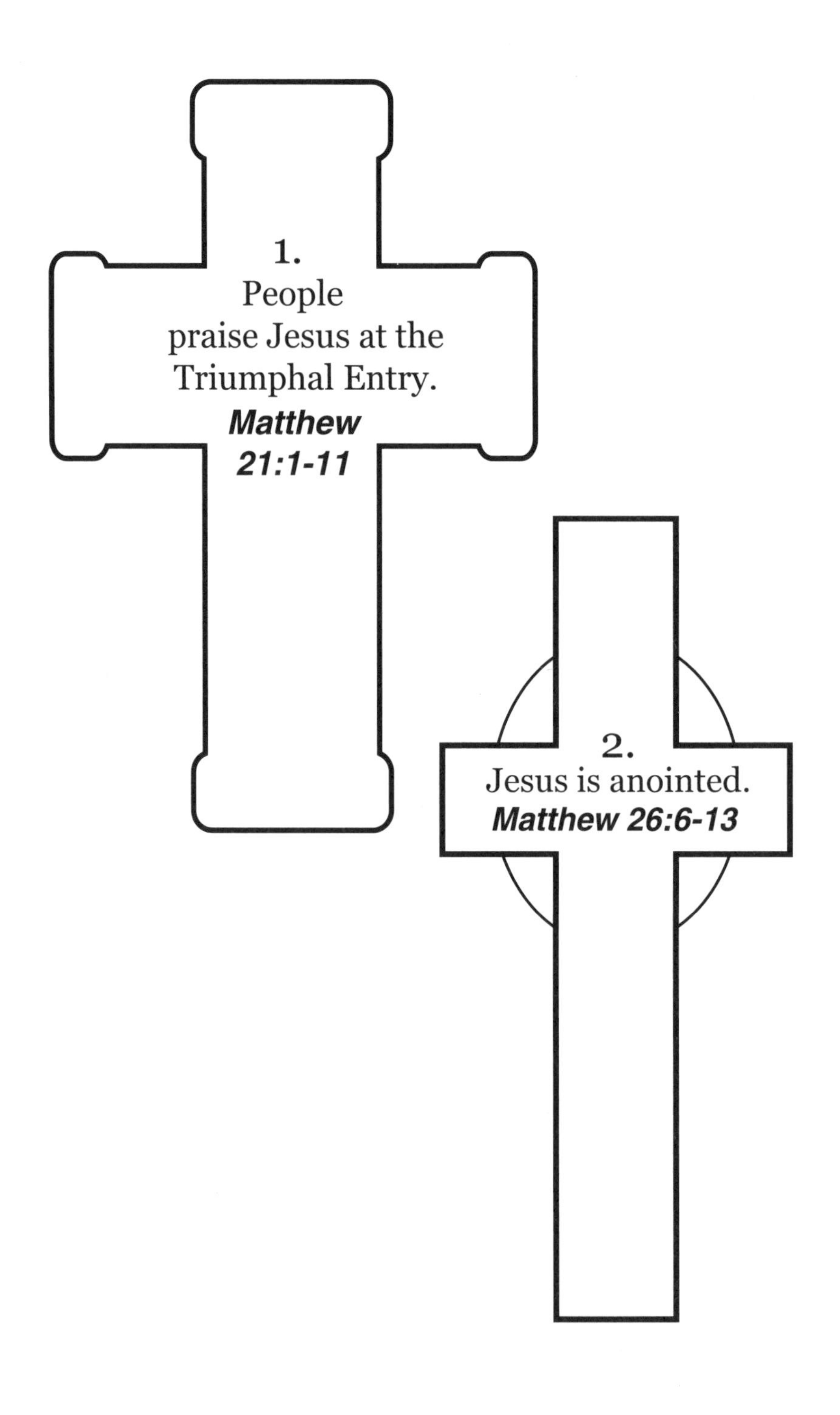

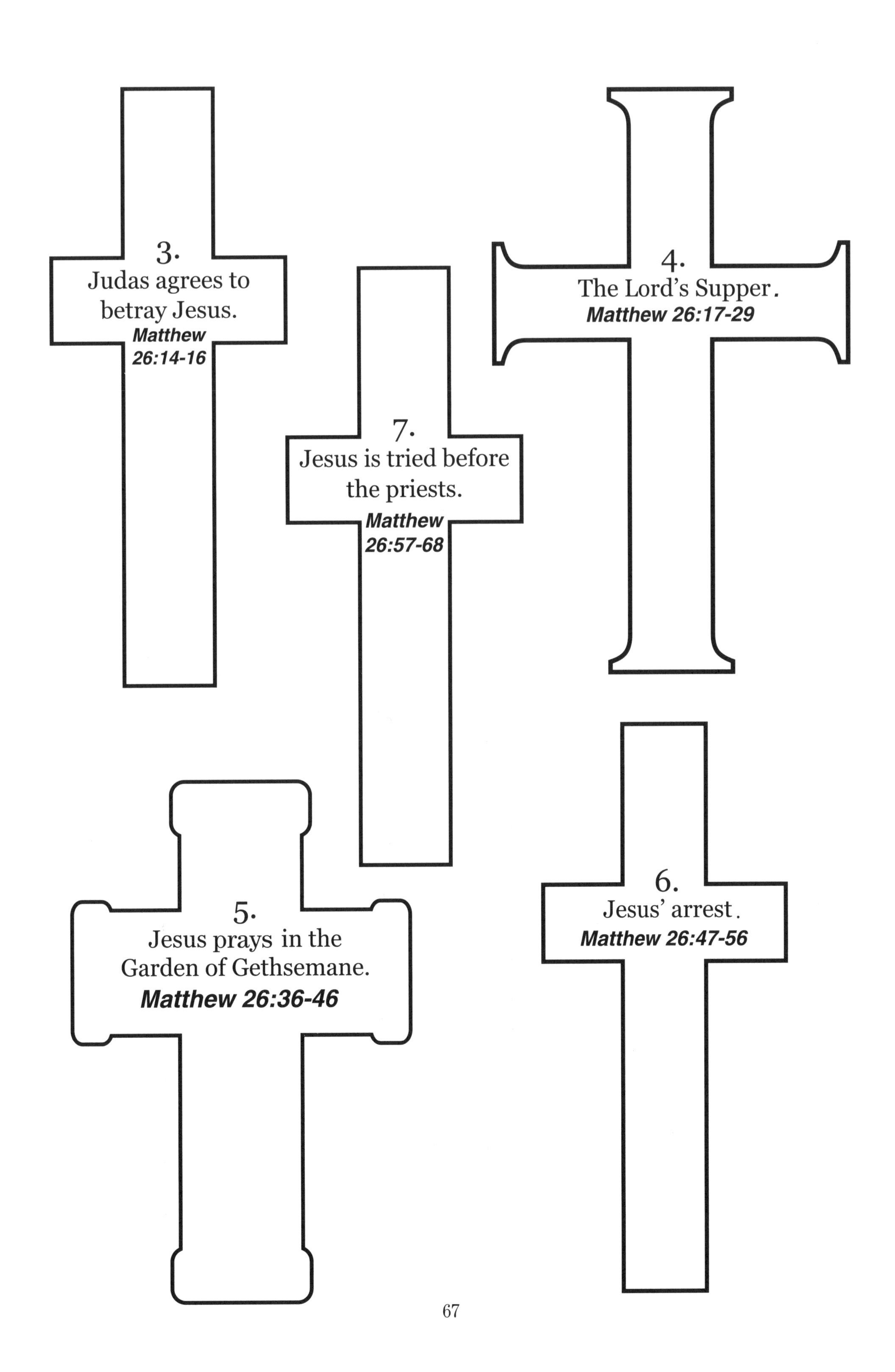
3.
Judas agrees to
betray Jesus.
Matthew
26:14-16
4.
The Lord's Supper.
Matthew 26:17-29
7.
Jesus is tried before
the priests.
Matthew
26:57-68
5.
Jesus prays in the
Garden of Gethsemane.
Matthew 26:36-46
6.
Jesus' arrest.
Matthew 26:47-56

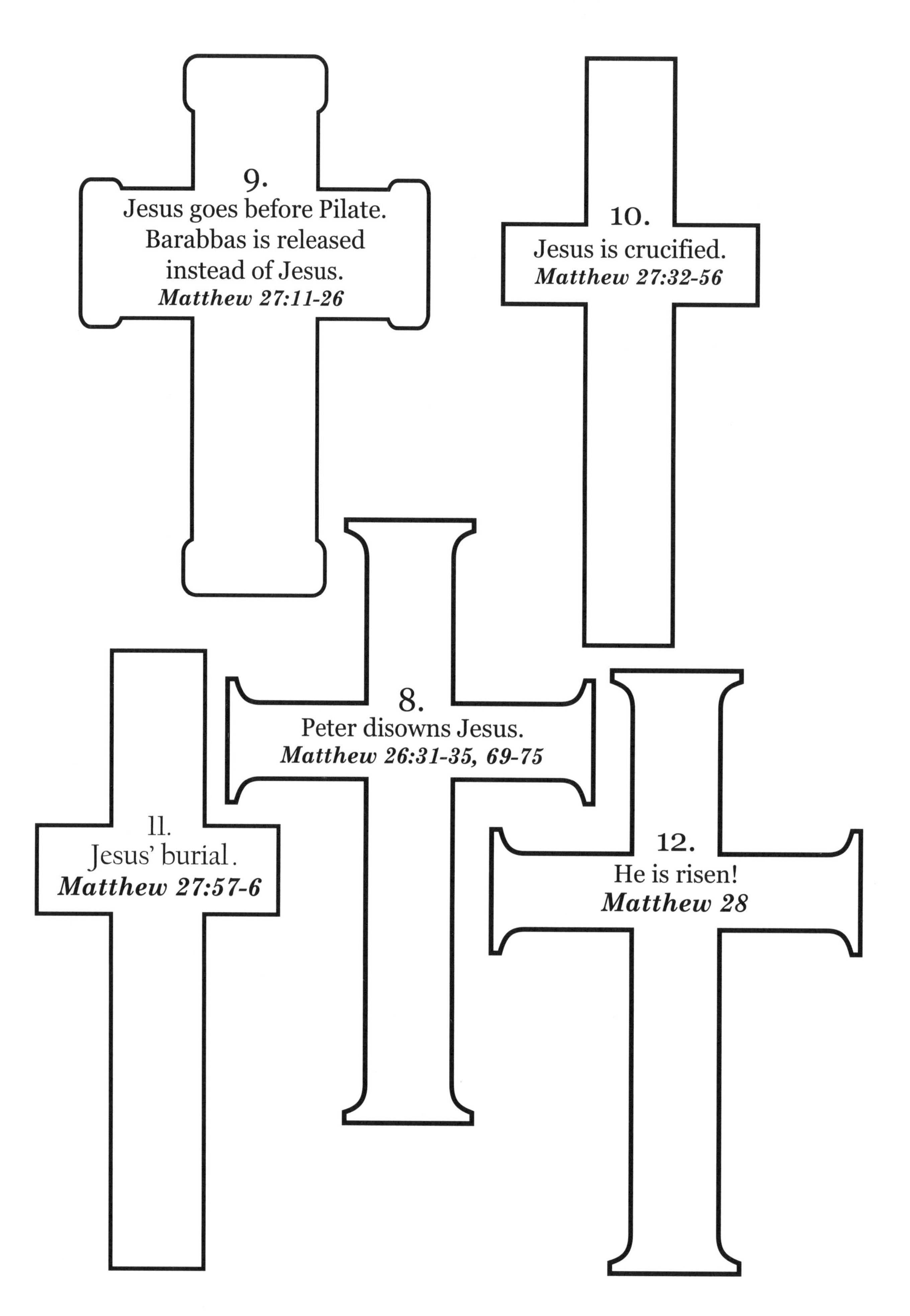
9.
Jesus goes before Pilate.
Barabbas is released
instead of Jesus.
Matthew 27:11-26
10.
Jesus is crucified.
Matthew 27:32-56
8.
Peter disowns Jesus.
Matthew 26:31-35, 69-75
11.
Jesus' burial.
Matthew 27:57-6
12.
He is risen!
Matthew 28

* Why? *

Th__s __s my bl__ __d

__f th__ c__v__n__t,

wh__ch __s p__ __r__d

__ __t f__r m__ny f__r

th__ f__rg__v__n__ss __f

s__ns. *—Matthew 26:28*

puzzle

WHAT YOU NEED

- duplicated page
- pens or pencils

WHAT TO DO

1. Give each student a puzzle page.
2. Say, **There is a very important reason that Jesus was crucified. Our Bible verses that tell the story also hold the key to why Jesus was crucified. Put the missing vowels in the verse to find out the reason.**
3. After the students have finished the puzzle, have them read the verse out loud together. Discuss the meaning of Jesus' dying for the forgiveness of our sins.

bulletin board

WHAT YOU NEED

- duplicated page
- junk mail CDs
- glue gun
- cardboard
- scissors

WHAT TO DO

1. Cut a large cross shape from cardboard. If you have a very large class, cut out more than one cross.
2. Have each student cut out and color a Jesus circle, then glue it to a CD.
3. Allow the students to take turns gluing their CDs to the cross shape (shiny side out) using a glue gun.
4. Say, **We can hang the cross in the church foyer for all to see. The lights will make it look like it is changing colors. What a beautiful way to remember Jesus' sacrifice for us!**

* Cross Display *

* Saved Arm Bands *

craft

WHAT YOU NEED

- duplicated page
- transparency sheets
- tape
- permanent markers
- scissors

WHAT TO DO

1. Before class, duplicate the patterns to transparency sheets.
2. Say, **We are going to make arm bands to wear or give to others. Each will say "Saved" to remind us that we have salvation through Jesus.**
3. Give each student a transparency sheet pattern. Each student should cut out a band along the dashed lines and tape the ends together at the back. Have the students color their arm bands with permanent markers.

craft

WHAT YOU NEED

- duplicated page
- craft sticks
- craft wire, various colors
- scissors

WHAT TO DO

1. Give each student a pattern page to show how to make the wrapped cross.
2. Give each student two craft sticks and about 6 yards of craft wire (you can cut it into smaller lengths for easier use).
3. Have each student cut about 1 inch off each end of one stick so both ends are flat.
4. Show how to wrap the cross. Begin with a long craft stick. Wrap wire around the stick from the top down about 1 inch. Wrap the wire around and around the stick, pushing the wraps close together to cover most of the stick.
5. At 1 inch down from top, add the cross bar (shorter ➢

The Way

* Wrapped Cross *

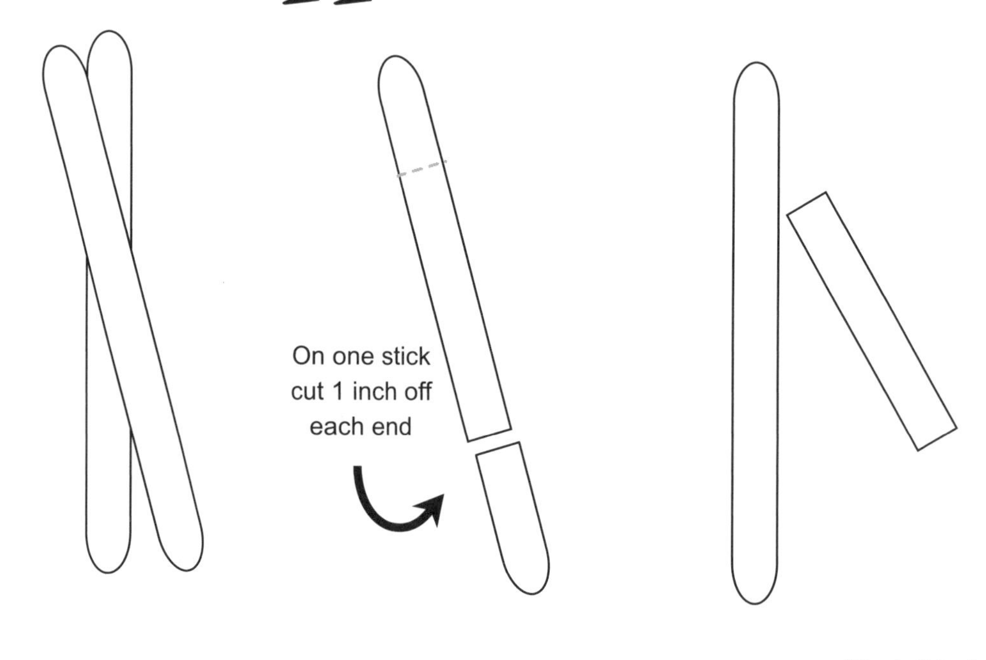

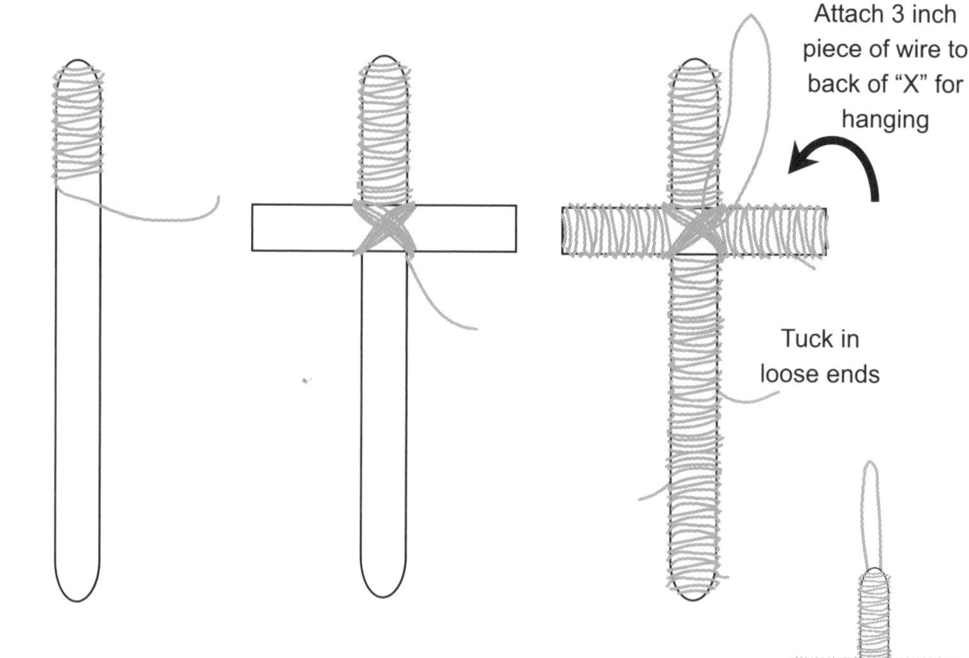

WHAT TO DO, CONTINUED

➢ piece of craft stick). Wrap wire in an X shape around the cross bar to hold. Then wrap the entire cross bar with wire.

6. Finish the cross by wrapping from under the cross bar to the bottom of the cross.
7. Weave in any loose ends.
8. Show how to make a loop from a 3-inch piece of wire and attach it to the back of the X holding the cross bar.

* Poem *

Jesus, the Ultimate Friend

Jesus, You mean everything to me.
Without You, where would I be?
You died on a cross to save my soul.
My life, my all, to You I owe.

____

____

____

express yourself

WHAT YOU NEED

- duplicated page
- pens or pencils

WHAT TO DO

1. Give each student a duplicated page.
2. Say, **Jesus made the ultimate sacrifice for each of us, and is the ultimate friend. He didn't give His life for just the other kids in class, or people elsewhere in the world...He gave it for you and for me! His sacrifice was for all, but it was also a very personal gift—the gift of forgiveness for our sins so that we can live with Him in heaven forever.**
3. Say, **Read the poem. Then think of some extra lines to add to the poem. Or write an entirely new poem, or even a prayer to thank Jesus for His love. Express yourself!**

• CHAPTER 8 •

Jesus Sends the Holy Spirit

MEMORY VERSE

But the Counselor, the Holy Spirit, whom the Father will send in my name, will teach you all things and will remind you of everything I have said to you. JOHN 14:26

* We're Not Alone *

Jesus was preparing His followers for what was about to happen: His death on the cross, His resurrection, and His ascension to heaven. The disciples had followed Jesus for a long time. Jesus knew they would feel lost after He was gone.

Jesus made the disciples a very special promise. "I will ask the Father, and he will give you another Counselor to be with you forever," He said, "the Spirit of truth."

He explained that the world would not be able to see the Holy Spirit, but the Spirit would live with and in each person. Not only would the Holy Spirit be there to comfort Jesus' followers, the Holy Spirit would teach them and remind them of all Jesus had taught.

"Peace I leave with you," Jesus said. "My peace I give you. Do not let your hearts be troubled and do not be afraid."

The Holy Spirit was not only for the disciples. Each of us has the Holy Spirit as a comforter, counselor, and guide, too. Jesus provided the Holy Spirit as one more way we can live happily as Christians.

BASED ON JOHN 14:15-31

Discussion Questions

1. Why do you think Jesus taught about the Holy Spirit?
2. Tell about a time you felt the Holy Spirit guiding you.

craft

Though We Don't See Him or Hear Him

WHAT YOU NEED

- pages 77 and 78, duplicated
- transparency sheets
- scissors
- rulers or 12-inch strips of wood or cardboard
- fishing line
- tape

WHAT TO DO

1. Give each student a copy of the two pattern pages duplicated to transparency sheets.
2. Have the students cut out the four clear shapes.
3. Say, **The Bible story is printed on the clear sheets to demonstrate the Holy Spirit's power. Although we cannot see the Holy Spirit, Jesus has promised to send the Holy Spirit to us. Let's learn more about what John 14:15-31 says about the Holy Spirit.**
4. Have the students hold each shape, one at a time, and read aloud what the shape says. The ➢

Holy Spirit

WHAT TO DO, CONTINUED

➢ shapes are numbered 1-4 so the students can read the lesson in the correct order.

5. Help the students turn the clear figures into a silent wind chime. Have each student cut four lengths of fishing line, about 8 inches long each. Show how to tape one of the clear figures to each of the lengths of fishing line and tie the four figures to a ruler or piece of wood or cardboard. Each student should tie a loop of fishing line to the top of his or her wind chime.
6. Say, **Our wind chimes are different than most. These are silent wind chimes. We can learn from the silent wind chimes that, although we cannot hear the Holy Spirit, the Spirit is really there.**

1.
Jesus prepared His followers for what
was about to happen:
His death on the cross, then His
resurrection and ascension to heaven.
2.
Jesus promised to send a
Counselor, the Holy Spirit, to
be with His followers. Jesus
explained that the world could
not see the Holy
Spirit, but the Spirit would
live within His followers.

4.
Every Christian also has the Holy Spirit as a
comforter, counselor,and guide. Jesus,
our Ultimate Teacher, taught us that we
would always have the Holy Spirit with us.
(John 14:15-31)
3.
The Holy Spirit would comfort,
teach, and guide. "Peace I leave
with you; my peace I give you,"
Jesus told them.
"Do not let your hearts be
troubled and do not be afraid."

* Holy Spirit Round *

song

Holy Spirit

Holy Spirit, Holy Spirit,
Jesus promised, Jesus promised,
You are my helper and guide,
You'll always be by my side.
God sent You.
God sent You.

WHAT YOU NEED

- duplicated page

WHAT TO DO

1. Give each student a copy of the song page.
3. Sing the song to the tune of "Are You Sleeping?"
4. Divide the class into two or three groups, and sing the song in a round.

puzzle

WHAT YOU NEED

- pages 80 and 81, duplicated
- pens/pencils

WHAT TO DO

1. Give each student a duplicated page.
2. Say, **Jesus made a promise to His disciples and to all believers. Now we are going to learn how Jesus fulfilled that promise.**
3. Say, **Beginning with the start arrow, write the word from the first row of each flame onto the blank lines of the other page. Follow the arrows around. When you reach the first flame again, go to the second line and write each word onto the blanks. Continue until you have written every word in the correct order to form the verses from Acts 2:1-4.**
4. Discuss the events in these verses with the students. Ask, **How did Jesus fulfill His promise?**

Holy Spirit

* Promise Fulfilled *

Acts 2:1-4

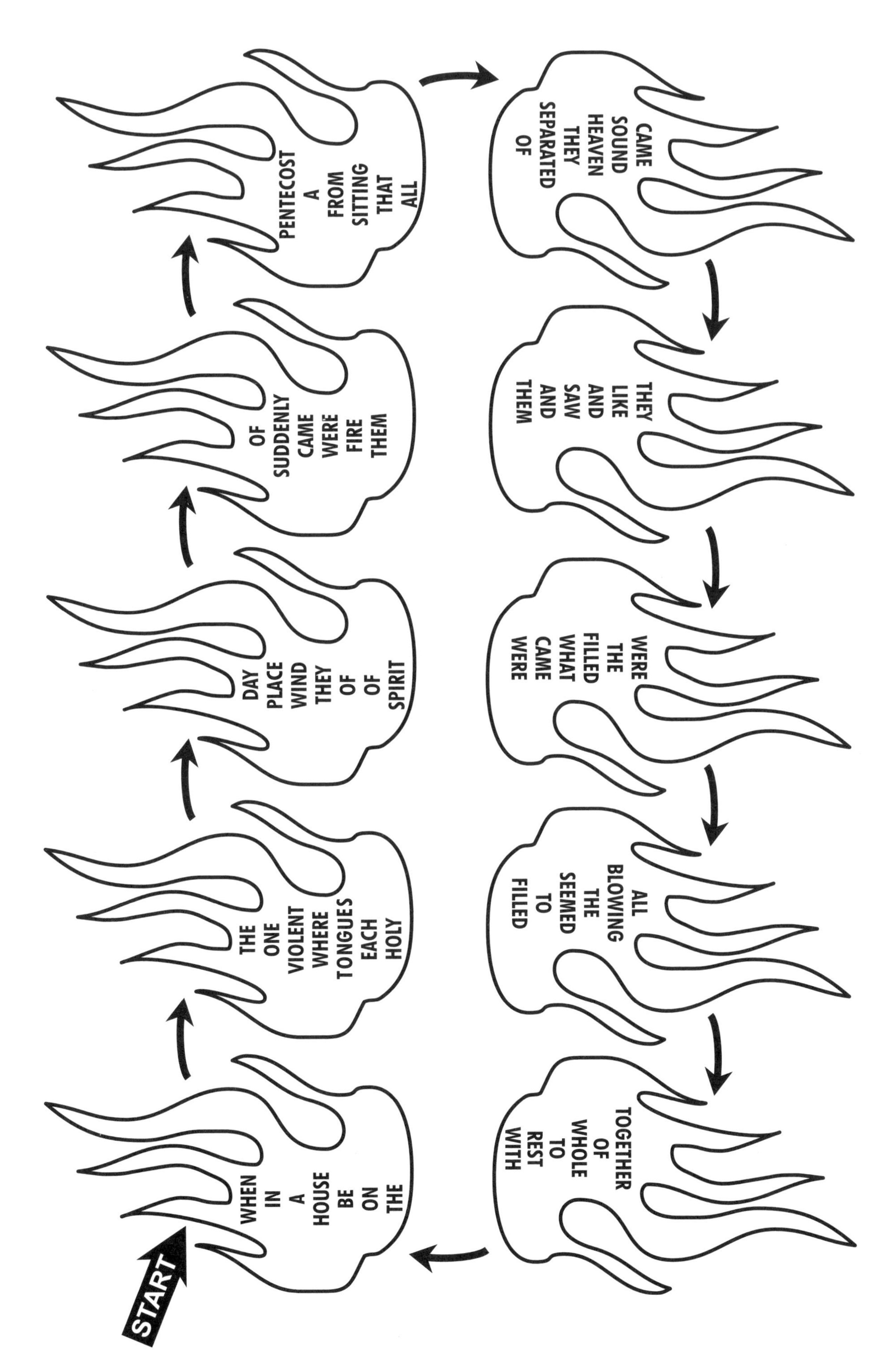
START
WHEN IN A HOUSE BE ON THE
THE ONE VIOLENT WHERE TONGUES EACH HOLY
DAY PLACE WIND THEY OF OF SPIRIT
OF SUDDENLY CAME WERE FIRE THEM
PENTECOST A FROM SITTING THAT ALL
CAME SOUND HEAVEN THEY SEPARATED OF
THEY LIKE AND SAW AND THEM
WERE THE FILLED WHAT CAME WERE
ALL BLOWING THE SEEMED TO FILLED
TOGETHER OF WHOLE TO REST WITH

craft

WHAT YOU NEED

- duplicated page
- glass jars or candle holders, about 3 inches tall
- glass paints
- glue
- scissors
- markers
- votive candles

WHAT TO DO

1. Give each student a pattern page.
2. Have the students cut the two Jesus ovals from the pattern pages.
3. Say, **You can paint your candle holders. Then color the Jesus ovals and glue them onto the sides of your candle holders. When you light the candles, you will be reminded that the Holy Spirit is our gift from Jesus, to be our counselor and our guide.**

Holy Spirit

* Holy Spirit * Candle Holder

* Travel Game *

games

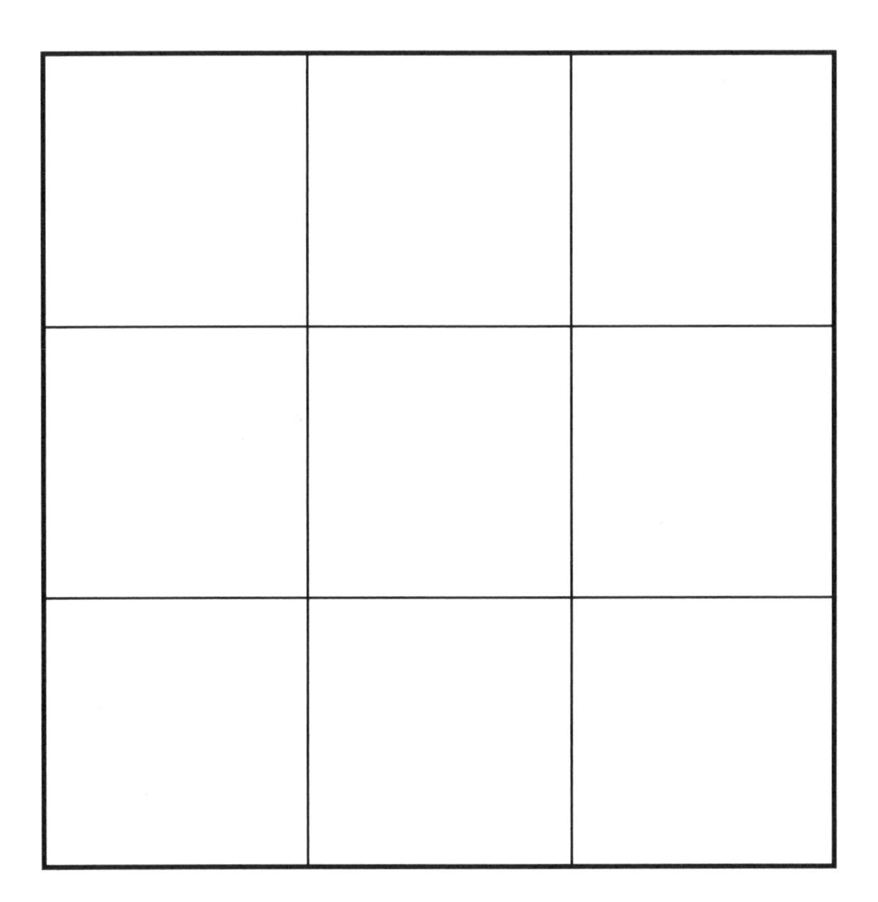

WHAT YOU NEED

- duplicated page
- CD cases
- glue
- 1 inch washers or wood rounds

WHAT TO DO

1. Give each student a duplicated page and CD case.
2. Say, **We are going to make a travel tic-tac-toe game in a clear CD case. The clear case will remind us that we have the Holy Spirit with us, even though we cannot see the Spirit. The game pieces will remind us that Jesus promised us the Holy Spirit.**
3. Have the students cut out the Jesus circles and the game squares.
4. Each student should glue the game square inside a CD case with the printed side of the paper facing up. Then each student should glue a game piece to each of the 10 washers or wood rounds.

Holy Spirit

group

* Receiving the * Spirit Relay

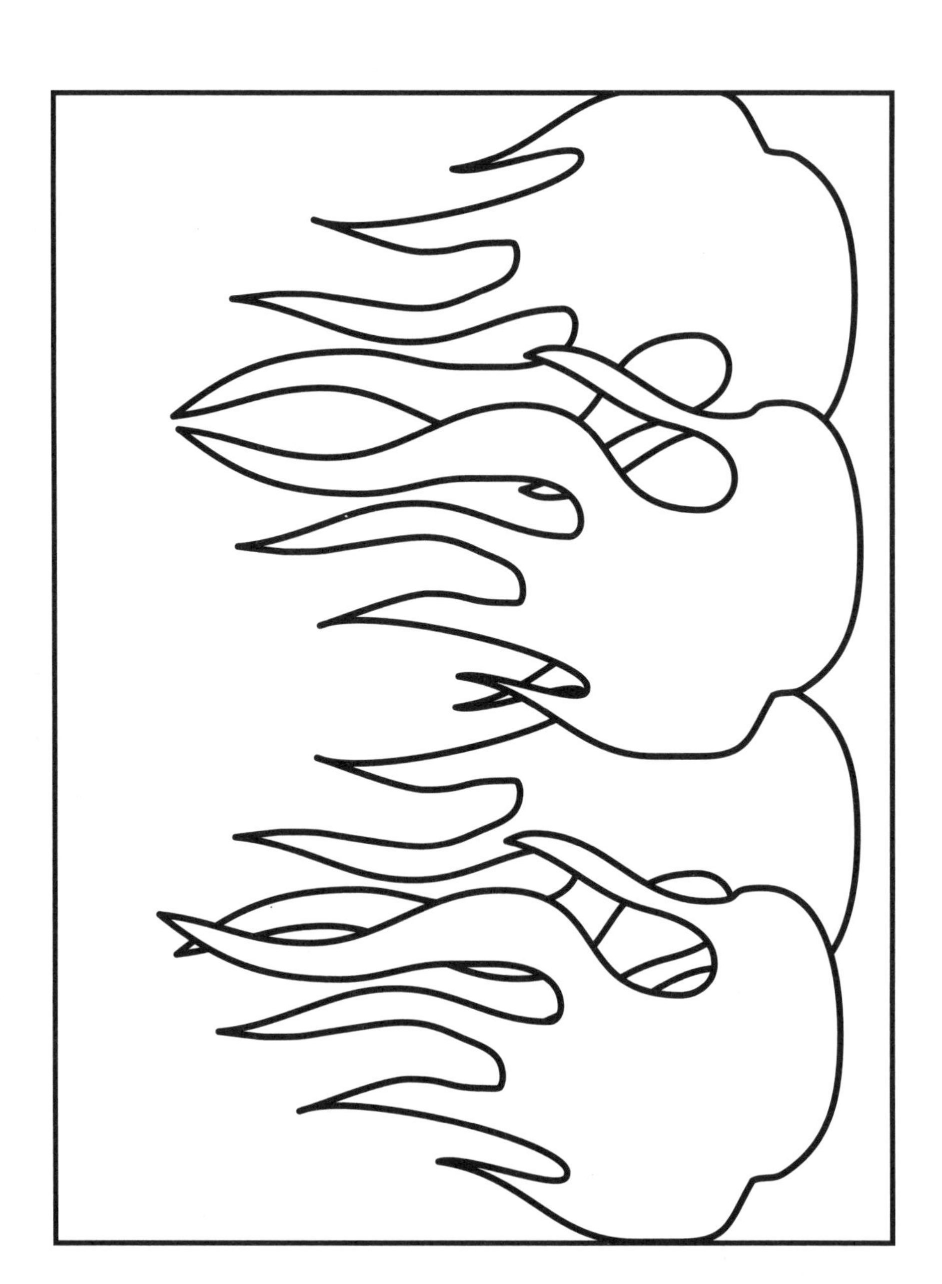

WHAT YOU NEED

- duplicated page
- toilet tissue tubes
- crayons or markers
- tape
- scissors
- markers

WHAT TO DO

1. Give each student a pattern page and a toilet tissue tube.
2. Have each student color and cut out the flame strip and tape it around the tissue tube.
3. To play the relay game, divide the class into teams. Have each team line up at one side of the room. Mark a spot across the room to where the teams will race.
4. Say, **When I say, "Go," the first person on each team should place a flame tube on his or her head. Go as quickly as you can to the finish line. You can keep your hands close to your flame, but not touching it, as** ➢

WHAT TO DO, CONTINUED

➢ **you walk. When you cross the finish line, the next member of your team can place a flame on his or her head and rush to the finish line.**

• CHAPTER 9 •

More Activities

craft

WHAT YOU NEED

- duplicated page
- scissors
- pens or pencils
- glue
- corrugated cardboard
- 3-inch vine wreaths
- purple ribbon
- hole punch
- twine

WHAT TO DO

1. Say, **You've probably sung "Jesus Loves Me." It might seem like a song for little kids, but it really has great meaning. All the lessons we have learned in this book point to the love Jesus has for us. Jesus shows His love and wants us to show that love to others.**
2. Give each student a pattern page. Have each student cut the cross from his or her page.

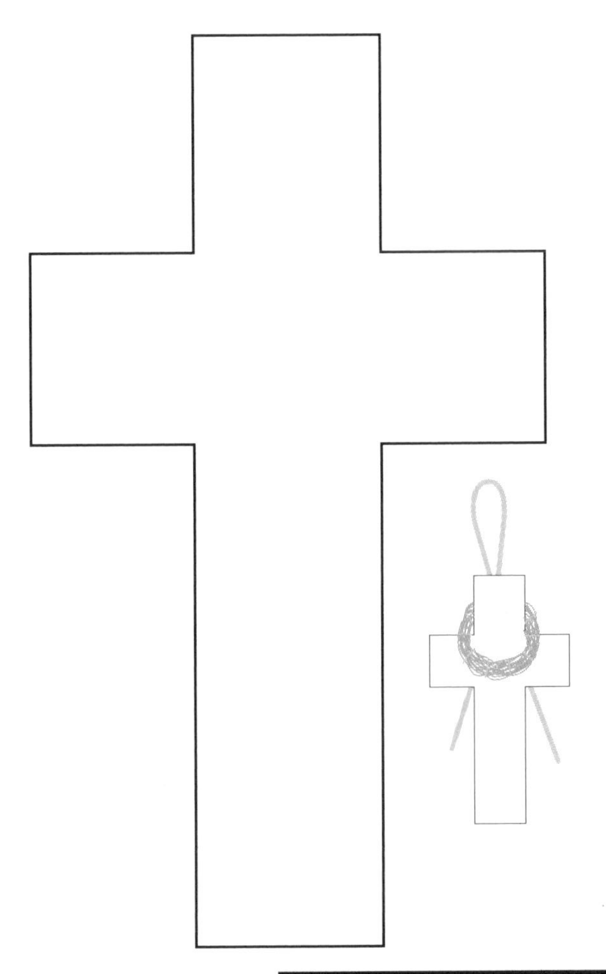

WHAT TO DO, CONTINUED

3. Show how to trace a cross on the smooth side of the corrugated cardboard, then cut out that cross.
4. Have the students turn their crosses to the corrugated sides.
5. Say, **Cut a 10-inch length of ribbon and drape it around the crossbars of the cross to represent the royalty of Jesus**.
6. Say, **Place a vine wreath over the crossbar of the cross to represent the crown of thorns placed on Jesus' head when He was crucified.**
7. Have each student glue his or her ribbon and crown in a couple of spots to hold them in place.
8. Instruct each student to punch a hole in the top of his or her cross with a hole punch, then thread a 6-inch piece of twine through the hole and tie for a hanger.

   Option: You can turn the hanging cross into a stand-up cross by placing clay into the bottom of a terra cotta planter saucer (around 3 inches), and pushing the bottom edge of the cross into the clay.

miscellaneous

express yourself

WHAT YOU NEED

- duplicated page
- markers
- plain paper
- paper fasteners

WHAT TO DO

1. Have the students use this journal cover for their "My Master's Plan" journaling pages from chapters 1-8.
2. Give the students extra plain paper so they can use their journals for further writing at home.
3. Show how to put the journals together by placing the cover on top and pushing two or three paper fasteners into the left edge. Bend the backs of the fasteners.

miscellaneous

* Journal Cover*

MY MASTER'S PLAN

* Expressions * Bracelets

Make a loop over your finger with the cord and form a circle, leaving a tail of about 2 inches.

Pull the circle off your finger.

Using the longer end of the cord, make a small loop and pull it through the circle.

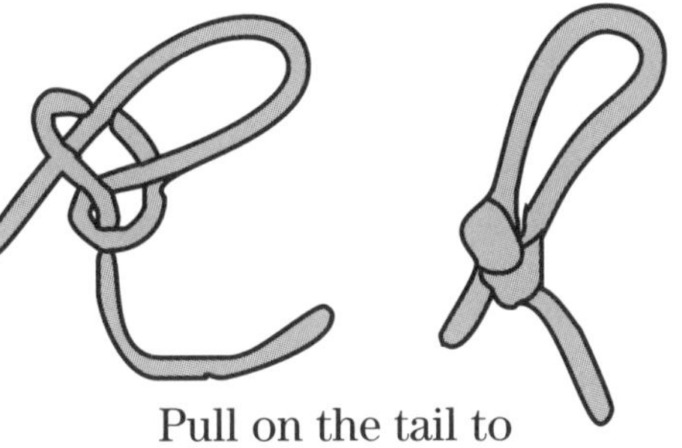

Pull on the tail to make the loop tight.

Continue pulling loops through the previous loop, as illustrated.

Every few loops, slip a bead over the loop before pulling a new loop through.

Make bracelet loose enough to slip onto your wrist.

craft

WHAT YOU NEED

- duplicated page
- craft cord, various colors
- letter beads
- symbol beads

WHAT TO DO

1. Say, **Wearing Christian jewelry is a great way to show your faith in Jesus. Let's make some bracelets and add Christian expressions and symbols to them.**
2. Have each student cut a 1-yard length of craft cord. The students can follow the directions on this page to make the bracelets. Some bead arrangements to suggest: WWJD (What Would Jesus Do); 4GIVEN; FROG (Fully Rely on God); HEAVENBOUND; SAVED; JESUS (HEART) ME; I (HEART) JESUS; PUSH (Pray Until Something Happens). The students also can use Christian symbol beads, and can add their names if they wish.

craft

WHAT YOU NEED

- pages 88 and 89, duplicated

WHAT TO DO

Try some of the following ideas:

1. Use the clip art and page borders as needed for bulletin boards (enlarged), letters to parents, church bulletins, or newsletters.
2. Copy the clip art pictures to plain paper. Let the students place shrink-art paper over the pictures of their choice and trace them for shrink-art designs. The students can color the art with markers and shrink it in a toaster oven for jewelry, backpack tags, or key chains.
3. Copy the artwork to colored paper. Let the students cut out the pictures they like and add them to scrapbook projects or journals.
4. Make greeting cards for the students to send or take to ➢

miscellaneous

Clip Art Pages

WHAT TO DO, CONTINUED

➢ nursing home residents, shut-ins, parents, another class, or someone who is ill. Duplicate the pages, then cut out some of the artwork to copy onto a sheet of paper, and quarter-fold it into greeting cards.

5. Enlarge the pictures to use as bulletin board borders. The students will enjoy coloring the border with markers as you share a lesson.

HOLY SPIRIT
SALVATION
FORGIVE

craft

Symbol Cross Mosaic

WHAT YOU NEED

- pages 90 and 91, duplicated
- card stock
- construction paper
- scissors
- glue
- yarn
- tape

WHAT TO DO

1. Give each student both pattern pages duplicated to card stock.
2. Say, **Our lessons have focused on Jesus. Use these symbol shapes to make a mosaic. Cut out the large cross first. Then cut out the other shapes from both pages. Arrange the mosaic pieces as you want. Use different colors of paper scraps to cut mosaic shapes. Then glue all the pieces to your cross.**
3. After the students have finished their crosses, instruct them to tape loops of yarn to the tops for hangers.

miscellaneous

group

* A Betrayal * and a Denial

WHAT YOU NEED

- duplicated page
- pencils

WHAT TO DO

1. Divide the class into two groups.
2. Say, **Jesus knew everything. He knew which of His disciples would betray Him and which would deny Him. Work together to find out as much as you can about the disciple your group is studying.**
3. Have the groups look up the Bible verses and write down what they find out about Judas and Peter.
4. Bring the class together and have each group's members present what they discovered. Also discuss how these situations are played out in our lives today.

Group 1 The Betrayal

Look up these verses:
Matthew 26:14-16, 21-25, 47-49
Matthew 27:1-9
Mark 14:10-11, 17-21, 43-46
Luke 22:1-6, 20-23
John 13:21-27
John 18:2-3

Who was the betrayer?

Did Jesus know who it was?

Did this man try to deny it?

Tell about how this man betrayed Jesus and how this made him feel later.

Have you ever betrayed Jesus?

What are some ways that we can betray Him?

How do you think our betrayal makes Jesus feel?

Group 2 The Denial

Look up these verses:
Matthew 26:31-35, 69-75
Mark 14:27-31, 66-72
Luke 22:31-34, 54-62
John 13:36-38
John 18:15-18, 25-27

Who was the one who denied Jesus?

How many times did he deny Jesus?

How did this man feel about what he had done?

Have you ever denied Jesus or acted ashamed that you believe in Him?

What are some ways we can deny Jesus?

How do you think Jesus feels when we deny Him?

miscellaneous

* Challenge Book *

CHALLENGE

Lesson title:

____

Where to find it in my Bible:

____

Words to look up in the concordance:

____

____

What I learned:

____

____

____

____

____

____

express yourself

WHAT YOU NEED

- duplicated page
- pens or pencils
- construction paper
- stapler
- Bible concordances
- duplicated story page for each lesson

WHAT TO DO

1. Give each student eight copies of the pattern page. Tape each story page to a table where the students can access them easily.
2. Say, **For each lesson in this book, look on the table at the story page. Write the title and verses for each lesson on one of the pages. The challenge is to find out more about each lesson.**
3. Say, **After you have done the challenge for each lesson, staple the pages together between two pieces of construction paper. Keep your Challenge Book**

WHAT TO DO, CONTINUED

➢ **to help you remember the lessons you've learned.**

miscellaneous

• ANSWER KEY •

My Master's Plan Answer Key

Page 8-9: Construct-a-Cartoon
I need to be baptized by You, yet You come to me?
This is my Son, whom I love; with Him I am well pleased.
Jesus was led by God's Spirit into the desert to be tempted by Satan.
After not eating for 40 days you must be very hungry. If You are really the Son of God, tell these stones to become bread.
It is written: Man does not live on bread alone, but on every word that comes from the mouth of God.
The devil took Jesus to the highest point of the temple and told Him to jump because the angels would catch Him.
It is also written: Do not put the Lord your God to the test.
I will give You all this, if You will bow down and worship me.
Away from me, Satan! It is written: Worship the Lord your God, and serve Him only!
Satan went away and angels came to take care of Jesus.

Page 13: Match the Verses
Matthew 4:4 — Deuteronomy 8:3
Matthew 4:6 — Psalm 91:11-12
Matthew 4:7 — Deuteronomy 6:16
Matthew 4:10 — Deuteronomy 6:13

Page 30: Compassion Acrostic
Care; Love; Meal; Help; Accept; Share; Visit; Give; Mission; Invite

Page 42: Instead of Worrying
star; elephant; octopus; fish; feather
Clue letters: FAITH

Page 52: Time for Forgiveness

My Master's Plan Answer Key

Page 61: Discover More

"For with the measure you use, it will be measured to you."
—Luke 6:38

Page 69: Why?
"This is my blood of the covenant, which is poured out for many for the forgiveness of sins."
—Matthew 26:28

Page 80: Promise Fulfilled
"When the day of Pentecost came, they were all together in one place. Suddenly a sound like the blowing of a violent wind came from heaven and filled the whole house where they were sitting. They saw what seemed to be tongues of fire that separated and came to rest on each of them. All of them were filled with the Holy Spirit."
—Acts 2:1-4